Negotiating Identities:

Adolescent Mothers' Journey to Motherhood

A RESEARCH STUDY

Kateresea L. Ford, PhD

BALBOA.
PRESS
A DIVISION OF HAY HOUSE

Balboa Press books may be ordered through booksellers or by contacting:

Balboa Press
A Division of Hay House
1663 Liberty Drive
Bloomington, IN 47403
www.balboapress.com
1 (877) 407-4847

Because of the dynamic nature of the Internet, any web addresses or links contained in this book may have changed since publication and may no longer be valid. The views expressed in this work are solely those of the author and do not necessarily reflect the views of the publisher, and the publisher hereby disclaims any responsibility for them.

The author of this book does not dispense medical advice or prescribe the use of any technique as a form of treatment for physical, emotional, or medical problems without the advice of a physician, either directly or indirectly. The intent of the author is only to offer information of a general nature to help you in your quest for emotional and spiritual well-being. In the event you use any of the information in this book for yourself, which is your constitutional right, the author and the publisher assume no responsibility for your actions.

Any people depicted in stock imagery provided by Thinkstock are models, and such images are being used for illustrative purposes only.
Certain stock imagery © Thinkstock.

Print information available on the last page.

ISBN: 978-1-5043-4981-9 (sc)
ISBN: 978-1-5043-4983-3 (hc)
ISBN: 978-1-5043-4982-6 (e)

Library of Congress Control Number: 2016901586

Balboa Press rev. date: 02/12/2016

CONTENTS

LIST OF TABLES

I dedicate this book to my beloved husband, Quo Vadis D. Ford, for not only being my confidant, cheering squad, and conductor of this personal journey, but also for being the wind beneath my wings. You fueled me with encouragement and inspiration, and I'm grateful for you being my light and guiding me through the cloudy days and dark times. Mostly, I appreciate you for listening and being there when I needed someone to listen to me and understand me.

Acknowledgments

I give the ultimate honor to God for the strength and power he bestowed on me to pursue and complete this journey

I would like to acknowledge the mothers and women in my life who gave me the power and strength to research and elaborate upon this valuable social topic. Those women were the epitome of leadership and strength, and they gave me the power and inspiration to strive to be both a good woman and a good mother. The power of motherhood often goes unrecognized and is terribly underrated.

I acknowledge my mother, Deborah Calhoun, who always inspired me to fight and to not accept what people gave me but rather to take charge, work hard, and take what I felt I deserved. I thank my sister, Chandra Gay, who is always my sounding board when the world gets on my last nerve. I thank my father, Carvin Calhoun, for instilling in me the idea of being a leader and not a follower and teaching me to always go for the gold, because failure is never an option. I thank my grandfathers, Chester Davis and Henry Calhoun, for the legacy they left me to admire as leaders and fighters against the unjust and unkind. I thank my grandmother, Mary Davis, for displaying and passing down her captivating energy and being the epitome of womanhood, motherhood, and family. The inspirational wisdom, power, and strength from her stories of triumph provide me with sparks to fuel my flame to be a fighter and to never allow anyone to keep me down—for when you are down, you have only one place to go, and that is *up*.

Lastly, I dedicate this project to all the teen mothers who were told that they were not going to amount to anything and neither would their children. I am living proof that this concept is not always true. These teen mothers have succeeded and risen above the prejudice and oppressive social system, and they have persevered long enough that they have not allowed themselves to become another statistic.

Kateresea L. Ford, PhD
Kateresea L. Ford

Introduction

It is difficult to be a teenage girl today. Young girls battle and compete to attain certain body types and fashion styles, and it's difficult for them to find their place in the teen universe. Becoming a mother in addition to all these challenges is yet another element. Teenage motherhood sparks many conversations filled with judgment, ridicule, and persecution for making that "one mistake" of saying yes!

That verbalized *yes* turns into forty weeks of disappointment, sorrow, judgment, fear, loneliness, and confusion. Those long months are followed by at least eighteen years of struggle, hardship, disappointment, loneliness, and often regret. Isn't it enough of a hardship to be a female teen in 2015? It's an even greater hardship to be a teenage mother in a society that even today brands her with a scarlet letter—reminding the young mother daily of how her decision caused a drastic change in her nuclear family and immediate circle of friends. Society casts off teen mothers with the high expectation of being good mothers.

I conducted this research on adolescent mothers as a co-owner (with my husband) of a residential group home for teen mothers. I have watched teenage mothers struggle with the emotional and psychosocial consequences of early childbearing. I have witnessed young mothers try to explain themselves to nonjudgmental and sympathetic listeners. I have watched them battle—mentally, emotionally, and psychologically—not sure of who they are and struggling with what they want to be, a teen or a mother. I have witnessed late-night crying bouts from these young ladies attempting to make sense of their messed-up worlds.

The disheartening part of watching these young ladies unfold and discover their new lives while professional and adults ridicule them and not offer moral support. The emotional turmoil takes a toll on these young mothers, and those feelings and emotions become internalized and absorbed into their personality and behaviors. The irony about these negative scenarios and situations is that some young mothers rise above all the negativity and are reborn as phoenix with brilliant and magical futures ahead of them.

Tales of empowerment and resilience are abundant in this marginalized population. Despite the negative looks and words they receive—and the blatant inhumanity and disrespect they get from adults and peers—these young women show fortitude, perseverance, and resilience, and they still make successful, positive strides in their lives. Although they may start with a rocky road of broken relationships, lack of support, or personal demons—they eventually find hope, set goals, and work to achieve their objectives as new mothers. Society argues that early childbearing causes strife in young teenage girls' lives, but some of the mother's note, "Becoming a mother saved my life!"

Before diving into this book, take off the glasses of prejudice and eliminate your personal perception of an oh-so-perfect childhood and upbringing. Put on the moccasins of each of these young ladies as they reveal their paradox of balancing two identities in two different worlds—teen and new mother—and starting their journey with no clue of what to do or where to go.

ABSTRACT

Negotiating Identities: The Transition to Motherhood
in Young Urban Adolescent Mothers

This study provides a description and understanding of the transitional experiences of urban adolescent mothers as they transformed into becoming mothers and developed maternal role identities. In addition, this study attempted to gather an understanding of the key factors and components that affected the urban adolescent mothers as they balanced the developmental duality of being a teen and becoming a mother. Through face-to-face, in-depth interviews, this researcher closely examined the perceptions, thoughts, feelings, and experiences of urban adolescent mothers regarding their emotions and feelings, parenting stressors, cognitive views of self, and environmental factors as they related to motherhood.

The study obtained a description and an understanding of the phenomenon these teenagers endured as they transitioned into their roles as mothers. It also identified the psychosocial impact that early childbearing had on their overall identity development. The sample populations used for this study consisted of urban adolescent mothers between the ages of 18 and 22 who resided in a southeastern urban city. Twelve mothers between the ages of 18 and 22 provided in-depth data revealing their experiences.

The results of this study identified six reoccurring themes shared by the participants: (a) experiencing conflicting identities, (b) defining a new and positive sense of self, (c) accepting maternal role duties and responsibilities, (d) constantly needing support, (e) experiencing emotional cycling, and (f) experiencing mental health symptomology. Furthermore, the findings suggest that the transitional process of adolescents becoming mothers consists of cognitive fluctuation. These might include the following: thoughts, feelings, and emotions about their new roles as mothers and contemplation of their roles as adolescents; behavioral transformation, which includes making decisions and taking more positive and goal-oriented actions; and the continual need for consistency, stabilization, and support to assist them with the psychological paradox of their dueling worlds of being adolescents and becoming a mothers. Further research should include a larger sample population and additional exploration of the emotional cycling process of adolescent mothers.

Chapter 1

INTRODUCTION

Introduction to the Problem

Adolescent mothers in the United States often lack maturity and the cognitive and emotional capabilities of parenting because of the interruption of the adolescent development phase and the early transition from adolescence to motherhood (Devito 2007; Sieger and Renk 2007). The act and the process of being a teen and then becoming a mother have not been adequately addressed in the research pertaining to adolescent mothers (Clemmens 2002; Holub et al. 2007; Hurlburt and McDonald 1997; Kaye 2008).

Early childbearing during the adolescent period causes a wavering effect on the development of self-identity and maternal-role identity in adolescent mothers (Holub et al. 2007; Kaiser and Hayes 2004). During adolescence, mothers endure natural and common dilemmas, such as exploring and examining their psychological characteristics and battling with who they really are and how they fit in to their social world (Larson 2004; Steinberg and Morris 2001).

The effects of early childbearing during the "self-seeking" period interrupt their current stage of identity development, which leads to the disruption of establishing a true sense of identity. In addition, adolescent mothers find themselves being forced to both establish and adjust to additional roles, including the challenge of developing a maternal identity that they are typically emotionally and psychologically unprepared to handle (Deutscher, Fewell, and Gross 2006; Hanna 2001; Oxford et al. 2005).

This disruption often leads to an adolescent mother's wavering between conflicting demands of simultaneously being a *teenager* and a *mother*. (Kaye 2008; Lesser, Oakes, and Koniak-Griffin 2003; Stiles 2010). This dualism has the potential to cause additional anxiety, uncertainty, and hopelessness.

Current literature reveals that adolescent mothers continue to struggle with the emotional factors often associated with early childbearing, such as depressive symptoms and lack of support (McDonell, Limber, and Connor-Godbey 2007). Due to common stressors of motherhood, some adolescent mothers have been found to inflict elevated levels of parental abuse on their children (Borkowski, Whitman, and Farris 2007; Lee 2009). Common and consistent findings in research on early childbearing show young mothers experience a loss of social connections with peers, a lack of emotional and financial support, and a disruption of their education; the result is often a failure to obtain a high school degree (Ventura et al. and National Center for Health Statistics, Centers for Disease Control and Prevention 2011).

There is, however, a noted gap in the literature pertaining to the process in which an adolescent mother transforms and accepts her role as a mother (Holub et al. 2007; Oxford, Lee, and Lohr 2010). Conclusions and implications in previous studies indicate a need for additional research addressing the issues of personal dynamics, emotional status, and cognitive processes that adolescent mothers experience during their transformation into motherhood (Kaiser and Hayes 2004; Oxford, Jungeun, and Lohr 2005; Sadler and Cowlin 2003).

Brubaker and Wright (2006) demonstrated in their qualitative study that urban African American adolescent mothers were able to cope with the transition to motherhood with the help and support of kinship and family members (e.g., their mothers). The researchers found family caregiving was not only a pertinent element in assisting mothers with identity development but also an important factor for the teens to become good mothers. Current research confirms that supportive adult figures—including adults in their family or adult mentors from organized programs (e.g., home visit or school-based programming providing daycare and parenting advice)—are positive, essential elements to assist young, urban African American mothers as they take on their new roles (DeSocio et al. 2013; Jones et al. 2007; Silk and Romero 2013). Klaw (2008) conducted a phenomenological study providing insight into the aspirations and expectations vocalized by many urban pregnant and parenting mothers. In the study, the pregnant participants also stated they were aware of the barriers they would face to finish high school and achieve economic mobility; however, the urban mothers continued to vocalize their aspirations and hopes for future educational and economic achievement.

Adolescent motherhood is not an uncommon practice; however, the dynamics of these mothers' transitions to developing maternal-role identity are understudied. Implications for additional research were identified in several studies regarding this specific topic. Rosengard et al. (2006) suggested that future qualitative studies utilize more in-depth interviews to better understand the complexities of both the advantages and disadvantages of teen parenting.

Brubaker and Wright (2006) also suggested in their qualitative research with fifty-one African American teen mothers that family caregiving not only provides the additional support needed to assist with identity transformation for the young mothers to become good mothers, but also it assists those who experienced the interruption to their childhood.

Holub et al. (2007) concluded that programs with an increased concentration of early interventions are needed to assist adolescent mothers with their maternal adjustment and to help them cope with—and reduce—their frequent emotional distress.

In reviewing one hundred studies that examined adolescent mothers, Noria, Weed, and Keough (2007) found they revealed developmental struggles (such as immature affective relationships) and hostile interactions with peers and family. These interactions had an impact "on the maternal development, which led to problematic maternal adjustment" (p. 44).

Background of the Study

Data reveal a continual need for services and intervention for adolescent mothers. According to Richmond, the city had an extremely high teen pregnancy rate. According to the Virginia state department of health, the City of Richmond had the fourth highest teen pregnancy rate in the state (Health Department 2012). The state teen pregnancy rate was 24.3 per thousand women ages ten to nineteen. In 2006, the National Campaign to Prevent Teen and Unplanned Pregnancy concluded that early teen childbearing cost Virginia $215 million.

The program found that 35 percent of costs were federal and 65 percent were state and local. The state's efforts to reduce the teen pregnancy rate in Virginia ultimately saved an estimated $205 million in 2008 (The National Campaign to Prevent Teen and Unplanned Pregnancy 2010 and 2014).

The study location continues to have one of the highest rates of teen pregnancy and nonmarital births within the state. Compared with the average state rate of 24.3 per thousand, the city's 2009 rate of resident teen pregnancy was 70.1 per thousand (Virginia State Department of Health (VDH), Center for Health Statistics [n.d]). According to a local community needs assessment conducted by the Community Foundation in 2008, the estimated public costs for live births to teens in 2004 in the central area of the state (where the study took place) was more than $19.7 million (Dunn 2008). The assessment also found that children of adolescent parents face greater risk factors than children born to older parents. Children born to teen parents are more likely to have multiple caretakers throughout their childhood and are 40 percent more likely to have a reported case of abuse or neglect (Community Foundation 2008).

The results of early childbearing can be problematic, and they can cause a host of ecological, social, and psychosocial issues for the teen mother. Developing, establishing, and accepting a maternal–role identity is often a professed problem for teen mothers, coupled with the lack of knowledge about how to properly provide nurturance, guidance, and support. This often results in the mother being highly stressed and in a state of confusion (Aiello and Lancaster 2007; Knoche, Givens, and Sheridan 2007; Sadler and Cowlin 2003). The major struggles endured by teen mothers have been found to lead to poor developmental, educational, mental, and social outcomes for themselves and their children (Hofferth and Goldschieder 2010; Oxford et al. 2005). Teen mothers are known to struggle with high school completion and obtaining financial stability (Lodgson et al. 2008). They have significantly higher levels of postpartum depression as well as depressive symptoms (Abrams and Curran 2011; Barnet, Liu, and DeVoe 2008; Eshabugh, Lempers, and Luze 2006; Lanzi, Bert, Jacobs, and Center for the Prevention of Child Neglect 2009). The daily stressors and responsibilities of motherhood, often leave the adolescent mothers in emotional distress (Lewin et al. 2011).

Researchers found that teen mothers struggle with understanding their role and in developing a maternal identity (Hallman 2007; Holub et al. 2007).

Oftentimes, teen mothers are emotionally conflicted between behaving as teens and taking on the responsibilities of an adult and parenting a child (Larson 2004), which causes a great deal of impatience, grief, regret, and hostility. These actions, emotions, and behaviors have led teen mothers to be more likely to abuse and neglect their children (Bert, Guner, and Lanzi 2009; Borkowski, Whitman, and Keogh 2007).

Unfortunately, young mothers living in urban areas have been found to suffer more because of reduced or absent resources, which are often associated with the normal characteristics of urban living (Goodman and Aber 2010). Ecological factors of urban living (such as financially unstable school systems, failing community and social service programs, and other limited resources) often result in a lack of opportunity to personally excel because of emotional and economic strains of adolescent motherhood. These economic and emotional strains make the transition from adolescence to motherhood a more difficult experience (Budd, Holdsworth, and HoganBruen 2006; Taylor 2011). This study was undertaken to provide a more in-depth and comprehensive understanding of the experiences that adolescent mothers endure during their transformation from an adolescent to developing and establishing their role as a mother.

Statement of the Problem

This study examined the experiences and the process of maternal identity development of urban adolescent mothers as they transitioned into motherhood. The experience of early childbearing by urban adolescent mothers includes high levels of anxiety (Budd et al. 2006), parenting stress (Larson 2004), depression (Abrams and Curran 2011; Barnet et al. 2008; Shanok and Miller 2007b), and the lack of significant cognitive and emotional abilities to adequately care for their children (Devito 2007; Sieger and Renk 2007). The complexities and numerous risk factors of urban living often put these adolescent women at risk for factors including poverty, lack of education obtainment, domestic and family violence, and lack of financial and supportive resources (Lipman, Georgiades, and Boyle 2011; Oxford et al. 2010). Knowledge about the psychosocial effects of interrupting the adolescent stage due to early childbearing is limited (Brubaker and Wright 2006; Hurlburt and McDonald 1997; Kaye 2008). In addition, little is known about the interruption of the adolescent stage and how it affects adolescent mothers' concepts of becoming a mother and their parenting attitudes (Hanna 2001; Lee 2009). The adolescent stage is the time when growth through self-reliance and self-identity prepare adolescents for the next stage of making imperative decisions and building self-esteem (Zastrow and Kirst-Ashman 2006). However, when the stage is interrupted and inundated with emotional and economic struggles, an underdeveloped sense of identity and role confusion can result.

The underestimated expectations of the duties and responsibilities of motherhood can make early childbearing problematic, not only for the adolescent mother but also for her child (Hunt, Joe-Laidler, and MacKenzie 2005). Understanding the psychosocial effects of early childbearing is crucial because the numbers of child abuse and neglect cases have been found to be increasingly high among young mothers as a result of poor parenting practices (Lee 2009).

Purpose of the Study

The purpose of this phenomenological qualitative study was to identify the perceptions, thoughts, feelings, and experiences of urban adolescent mothers regarding their: (a) levels of anxiety, (b) parenting stressors, (c) self-identity, and (d) emotions as they relate to their process and transition into motherhood. Early childbearing has been shown to have a significant impact on the cognitive and emotional behaviors of young mothers (Brehey and Stephens 2007). Cox et al. (2008) found that teen mothers' high levels of depressive symptoms were associated with decreased maternal caretaking capabilities and decreased levels of social support.

Cox et al. also found that emotional factors such as anxiety and depression were associated with decreased maternal confidence and the mother's inability to parent, which resulted in a perceived decrease in maternal social support. This perceived decrease in maternal social support affected overall maternal self-esteem. In addition, Reid and Meadows-Oliver (2007) found similar results with teen mothers experiencing lower levels of social support, decreased self-esteem, and increased conflict with family. These factors relating to teen mothers increased the levels and rates of depression during their first postpartum year.

Rationale

Early childbearing has potentially negative effects and outcomes for both the mother and her offspring (Borkowski, Whitman, and Farris 2007; Milan et al. 2004; SmithBattle and Leonard 2012). Accounting for the psychosocial factors and understanding how adolescent mothers embrace their new role as mothers will be essential in planning and establishing more suitable and reputable preventive and transition-enhancing interventions for young single mothers. Currently, this research area has failed to be fully developed (Hurlburt and McDonald 1997; Kaye 2008). A primary risk factor often mentioned in research relating to early childbearing is the element of parenting.

Parenting without the proper cognitive and emotional state of mind, without role understanding, and without a certain level of maturity lends to the high numbers of abuse and neglect cases suffered by children of adolescent mothers (Bert et al. 2009; Lee 2009; Lounds, Borkowski, and Whitman 2006).

Early childbearing during adolescence can be problematic to a teen mother due to incomplete identity development during the adolescent stage. This makes it difficult for her to manage the cognitive and emotional expectations and responsibilities of parenthood (Meyer, Jain, and Canfield-Davis 2011). Teenage parents have not had an opportunity to fully explore and resolve their own inner conflicts and have not adequately developed a full understanding of their roles, established an identity, or had life experiences outside of being a teen (Oxford et al. 2005).

Adolescent mothers continue to struggle with the emotional factors often associated with early childbearing, such as depressive symptoms and lack of support (McDonell et al. 2007). Many adolescent mothers are unable to obtain a high school diploma, which leads to low-wage employment or unemployment; this can further lead to financial difficulties and even criminal activities (Coley and Chase-Lansdale 1998; Furstenburg, Brooks-Gun, and Morgan 1987; Letourneau, Stewart, and Barnfather 2004; Whitman et al. 2001).

For years, teen pregnancy has been deemed as a negative factor affecting our country's social, economic, and physical health (Meyer et al. 2011). Numerous studies have documented the outcomes and results of early childbearing. Although historical research often paints a negative picture of adolescent motherhood, current research suggests that adolescent mothers experience the same transitional factors to parenthood as older women (Lashay, Hans, and Henson, 2009). Previous qualitative studies conducted on adolescent mothers revealed the positive changes that early childbearing had on the adolescent mother's life (Klaw 2008). Lashay, Hans and Henson (2009) studied the transitions to motherhood in African American adolescent mothers; they found the mothers took pride in their children and viewed their relationships with their babies as important. Shanok and Miller (2007a) found urban African American adolescent mothers felt that having a baby—even though it was unplanned—was positive because it made them have a different perspective on life.

Research has revealed the negative effects early childbearing has on the young mother, but there appear to be positive elements resulting from the unplanned birth. Young mothers gain maturity, responsibility, and increased self-awareness and selfworth (Deutcscher, Fewell, and Gross 2006; Easterbrooks et al. 2010; Furstenberg 2003). In addition, research suggests that young mothers living in urban areas often lack resources and support, which tends to lead to high stress and depression (Borkowski, Whitman, and Farris 2007). However, some research suggests that early childbearing results in positive changes for young mothers who once engaged in antisocial activities, such as drug and alcohol abuse and risky sexual behaviors (Jacobs and Mollborn 2012; Lesser et al. 2003; Shanok and Miller 2007; Wright and Davis 2008). The positive changes stemmed from the young mothers arriving at a point in their lives where they began to experience elevated self-esteem (Edin and Kefalas 2005), began to make better decisions for themselves, and starting thinking about future outcomes for their babies (Hope, Wilder, and Watt 2003; Swedish et al. 2010).

Brubaker and Wright (2006) demonstrated in their qualitative study how urban African American adolescent mothers were able to cope with their transition to motherhood with the help and support of kinship and family members (such as mothers), and knowing they had support and resources eased transitional stressors for the mothers.

Outcomes from this study could provide support for additional funding and resource options to assist adolescent mothers in eliminating the backlash often linked to and influenced by early childbearing: high school dropout rates, unemployment, crime, and repeated unplanned pregnancies. In addition, the increased responsibilities and duties of early parenting have been found to cause elevated levels of stress and frustration, which can lead these young mothers to abuse their children (Lee 2009). In these situations, additional support can be beneficial not only for the adolescent mother but also for her child.

The study could affect the field by establishing an understanding of the perceptions, thoughts, feelings, and experiences adolescent mothers experience during their transition from being a teenager to becoming a mother. The psychosocial factors influence the transition from adolescence to motherhood, and current research lacks the focus on the phenomenal elements of transforming from being an adolescent to developing a maternal-role identity (Kaye 2008; Kaiser and Hays 2004; Lesser et al. 2003). Results from this research could shed light on the process of maternal identity and maternal role development as adolescent mothers transition into motherhood. In addition, the results could provide a better understanding of the influences and effects early childbearing has on the psychosocial development of adolescent mothers, as well as the ecological factors affecting transition to motherhood (Easterbrooks et al. 2010). The vulnerabilities of adolescent mothers challenge the prevailing assumptions that they are emotionally and mentally capable of properly parenting their children (Easterbrooks et al. 2010).

Currently, Virginia's public health department offers teen parents a program that assists them with children up to the age of two years. Currently there are no public services specializing in counseling, parenting, or transitional programming for adolescent mothers. The outcomes from this study could substantiate the fact that adolescent mothers struggle with the emotional and psychological effects of early childbearing. This is the result of an interrupted adolescent stage of development leading to the adolescent mothers' being cognitively incapable of successfully parenting their offspring. This understanding could lead to allocation of government resources for additional psychosocial and psycho-educational services to assist adolescent mothers beyond the basic public health and social service programming and services currently available.

The findings from this study could support the needs of adolescent mothers for postpartum clinical counseling and consultation; this would assist them during their emotional and psychological adjustment. Clemmens (2002) found that adolescent mothers experience posttraumatic stress symptoms from labor and delivery along with feelings of social isolation and abandonment. However, there has been an increase in the number of studies investigating posttraumatic stress disorder (PTSD) relating to postpartum stress and mental health after giving birth (Ammerman et al. 2012; Sumner et al. 2011).

Results from this study could provide avenues to eliminate possible repeat pregnancies as well as establish more effective methods of teen pregnancy prevention. Finally, the outcomes from the study could assist in advocating for additional state funding and programming to assist adolescents with their transition from being teens to becoming mothers by providing proper education and outreach services.

Research Questions

The study addresses the following research questions:

> RQ1: How do teen mothers develop maternal-role identity?

> RQ2: How do teen mothers describe the experience of transitioning from being a teen to being a teen mother?

Significance of the Study

The results from this research provide a more defined understanding of the perceptions, thoughts, feelings, and experiences of urban adolescent mothers as they transition from being a teen to becoming a mother. In addition, this study attempts to establish a more defined understanding of the psychosocial effects of early childbearing, its impact on the adolescent mother's dual development of self-identity and maternal identity, and how it affects her ability to parent. The research addresses specific topics explored in previous research, such as Mercer's theory of becoming a mother (BAM) (1985).

The research also expands on the preliminary works of Kaiser and Hays's (2004) Adolescent Prenatal Questionnaire (APQ) created for pregnant adolescent mothers. In this case, four psychosocial elements were examined and applied to adolescent mothers who had already given birth, and the impact of the transition to motherhood was evaluated. Understanding the psychosocial elements of the transition to motherhood could lead to policy makers, public health officials, and others providing services to or for adolescent mothers. It could help establish more relevant supportive services to assist mothers with cognitive and emotional challenges often associated with parenting. Current research lacks focus on psychosocial factors and the influence these factors have on the transitional process from adolescence to motherhood (Kaye 2008). Accounting for the psychosocial factors in research could be essential in planning and establishing more suitable and reputable preventive and transition-enhancing interventions for young single mothers.

Results from previous studies assert the need for more refined research and expansion of current theories (Kaiser and Hays 2004; SmithBattle 2007) and practices related to the transition into motherhood for teen mothers (Brubaker and Wright 2006; Holub et al. 2007; Noria et al. 2007; Rosengard 2006).

The state offers a program called Resource Mothers, a home-based visiting program that assists young mothers up to the age of nineteen with children younger than eighteen months.

The lack of programs and lack of focus on assisting adolescent mothers during their transition have left a detrimental gap in a needed service area in the state. This notion has left a much-needed service underused and a population of mothers struggling with their new responsibilities and duties. Establishing and funding programs that assist teen mothers from a more comprehensive, emotional, and ecological point of reference could lead to better outcomes of positive parenting. The vulnerabilities of teen mothers often challenge the prevailing assumptions that they are emotionally and mentally capable of properly parenting their children (Easterbrooks et al. 2010).

For years, teen pregnancy has negatively affected the country's social, economic, and physical health (Meyer et al. 2011). Numerous studies have documented the outcomes and results of early childbearing (Coley and Chase-Lansdale 1998; Driscoll et al. 2005; Furstenberg et al. 1987; Henretta 2007; Taylor 2010; Whitman et al. 2001), which often resulted in negative outcomes. The results from this study provide additional knowledge on the effects of early childbearing and the effects that transition has on the adolescent mother. This knowledge could be used to expand on current programs and educational services offered by local public health departments.

The results from this study could be used to substantiate that teen mothers struggle with the emotional and psychological effects of early childbearing, which is the result of an interrupted adolescent stage of developmental. This in turn can cause teen mothers to be cognitively incapable of parenting their offspring. This finding would enable state policy makers or additional academic programs to conduct more in-depth and empirical research on the psychological effects of adolescent childbearing. Based on a review of the literature on adolescent motherhood and the psychosocial effects of early childbearing, few studies have focused primarily on the psychological effects or effects of the interruption of the adolescent stage of development on the teen mother's psyche, thought process, and how they correlate with parenting attitudes and behaviors (Brubaker and Wright 2006; Hallman 2007; Hurlburt and McDonald 1997; Kaiser and Hayes 2004; Kaye 2008; Noria et al. 2007; Oxford et al. 2005; Rosendgard et al. 2006; Sadler and Cowlin 2003).

This research study expanded on the seminal research conducted by Hurlburt and McDonald (1997), one of the first studies to examine the multidimensional levels of adolescent parenthood, including examining the transition of adolescence to motherhood, the disturbance of adolescence and role identity, and the effects of the transition.

Results from this study could provide an opportunity for researchers to obtain a more comprehensive understanding of the experiences of urban adolescent mothers as they transition and develop their maternal-role identity. Although some limitations hindered the research, the results provide ample data for understanding specific feelings, thoughts, and perceptions that adolescent mothers endure as they transition into motherhood. In addition, the data from this research warrant further exploration of the cognitive effects early childbearing has on adolescent mothers and the emotional symptomology they experience after giving birth. Finally, this research unveiled the ongoing trials and tribulations often faced by unwed urban teen mothers when they are bestowed with the responsibility of raising a child.

Definition of Terms

For the purpose of this study, the following terms were used and defined:

> *Adolescent mother, teen mother, and young mother* are all used interchangeably and are defined as a woman who is marked by the onset of puberty, is between the ages of ten and twenty-three, gives birth to a child, and assumes the role of a mother (Borkowski, Whitman, and Farris 2007).

Psychosocial development refers to the process by which focus is placed on emotional maturity, relationships with others, and the ability to insert oneself in his or her environment (Blocher 2000).

Urban refers to "urbanized areas of 50,000 or more population and urban clusters of at least 2,500 and less than 50,000 population" (US Department of Commerce, Census Bureau 2011).

Assumptions and Limitations

The theoretical assumptions used for this study related to the psychosocial developmental struggles adolescent mothers endure during the adolescent stage of development. The researcher made the assumption that the participants were in the appropriate stage of development during the research study. The appropriate stages of development were aligned with theoretical frameworks used.

The first assumption involved the effects of early childbearing on the interruption of the adolescent stage of development according to Erikson's psychosocial development theory (Erikson, 1968). Adolescent mothers struggle with the disruption of their adolescent development and are thrust into duties and responsibilities of being mothers, causing the evolution of single identity development into a dualistic identity of being a teen and a mother simultaneously. The second assumption related to psychosocial elements, such as how emotions and self-esteem affect the transitional process as adolescents become mothers. A third assumption was that participants would be honest and candid during their interviews. The final assumption was that adolescent mothers would establish methods of coping with their newfound identity, duties, and responsibilities that differed from those of traditional mothers.

The participants had to recall their personal experiences, and it was assumed they were willing to remember and share all of their emotions and behaviors during their transition. Reconstruction of recalled memories could lead to the participants' including biases of their current situation and not divulging pertinent elements of their past. The possible lack of trustworthiness was a major threat and a limitation. The participants could have said what they thought the researcher wanted them to say or wanted them to think was the "correct response" without disclosing the facts. The study described the transitional process from the perspective of an urban adolescent mother at a time when she recognized that some of her behaviors were not appropriate. She may not have been willing to disclose the true situation or scenarios that occurred.

The researcher ensured the participants' confidentiality by providing them code names for identification; only the researcher had access to a list with all of the participants' original names. The demographic information and interviews were kept in a locked file cabinet in the researcher's office. The transcribed interviews were kept on a computer secured with two access passwords. The researcher also took a nonjudgmental approach and provided an explanation of the significance of the study, which avoided the possibility of any incorrect information being conveyed.

Limitations of this study were those often found with qualitative research—the issues of commitment and trustworthiness. The emotional content of the interview questions required the adolescent mothers to rehash their personal experiences, actions, and behaviors during the transitional phase of becoming a mother, and this process may have caused emotional turmoil for some of the participants. Providing a nonconfrontational approach—in addition to establishing and maintaining a rapport with the participants before the interview— helped alleviate the participants' apprehension (Leedy and Ormrod 2010). Furthermore, Capella University's Institution Research Board (IRB) considers the adolescent mother population to be a vulnerable population, and precautions in working with this population were required. For example, a state-licensed professional counselor was onsite during each interview to ensure that if the participants became overwhelmed with emotions, a professional was available to help them emotionally stabilize. The many limitations in working with this population include their transiency, disorderly lives, developmental levels, concerns about adequate childcare, and issues with transportation (Kaiser and Hays 2006).

To address the issues of credibility and quality often found in phenomenological research, the study used procedural safeguards and strategies to enhance both its quality and credibility. The credibility began with the expertise and knowledge of the researcher who is familiar with the adolescent mother population (Bloomberg and Volpe 2008). At the time of the study, the researcher had ten years of experience working with the adolescent mother population; she is also a state board licensed professional counselor.

Working with the vulnerable population of adolescent mothers required efficient planning due to the wavering decisions and daily disparities adolescent mothers often make. Understanding the population allowed the researcher to be equipped for any possible changes or unpredictable actions.

Another weakness of this study is that it was restricted to urban adolescent mothers, which limits the ability to apply the results to regional or statewide issues concerning adolescent mothers. To avoid upsetting the participants when they discussed their negative experiences, the researcher had a plenary questioning session during the initial contact. During this session, the potential participant expressed interest in the research. During the preliminary screening, the researcher asked the potential participant questions about her transition to determine whether the participant was a good candidate for the study. The researcher also used a nonconfrontational approach to assist with the difficult questions; this also helped establish and maintain a rapport with each participant (Leedy and Ormrod 2010). The interview questions were also field tested by three doctoral-level researchers and one licensed professional counselor, who were all familiar with this area of research. The interview questions were examined and checked for validity. The field study resulted in changing the language of the questions to an eighth-grade reading level.

The following section provides full details and explanations of the three frameworks used for the study: psychosocial development theory (Erikson 1968), BAM (Mercer 2004), and the conceptual model (Kaiser and Hays 2004).

Theoretical/Conceptual Framework

The theoretical assertions used for this research study were derived from the psychosocial development stages posed by Erikson's (1968) psychosocial development theory, Kaiser and Hays's conceptual model (Erikson 1968; Kaiser and Hays 2004), and Mercer's BAM (Mercer 2004) used to examine significant parallels of the transitional phenomena of becoming a mother. The results from this study can be applied to the current minimal empirical research on the psychosocial development and phenomenon of maternal-role identity development in early childbearing. They can also provide implications for future research inferences and development of models for adolescent mothers. This could include and incorporate more comprehensive interventions and transitional factors.

Adolescent mothers have found that their new roles of being a parent often results in great amounts of stress as well as social and emotional instability (Logsdon et al. 2008). The psychosocial adjustments cover clinical depression (Knoche et al. 2007) and the personal challenges of parenting, including social isolation, minimal support, and physical exhaustion (Birkeland, Thompson, and Phares 2005). All of these factors were found to significantly affect adolescent mothers' parenting attitudes and behaviors. Research has identified adolescent mothers' struggles with the transition to motherhood, and these struggles continue into adulthood (Eghan 2007; Noria et al. 2007).

Kaiser and Hays (2005) found that many psychosocial factors affect the transitional period to teen motherhood; teen mothers often endure periods of depression during the prenatal and postpartum periods. Mercer's (1985) maternal role attainment theory and Kaiser and Hays's (2005) theory contended that maternity identity is influenced by developmental aspects such as personality traits and the mother's self-concept. An example of this is the mother's ability to show empathy toward her child and to be flexible. Achievement of maternal role development has been a challenge for teen mothers due to psychosocial immaturity, lack of parenting skills, lack of cognitive ability to recognize developmental expectations of infant immaturity, and marital status (Mercer 2004).

Mercer also found that circumstantial factors such as poverty, low educational attainment, and lack of social support directly affect the process of developing into a mother (Mercer 2004). An additional theoretical framework used for this study consisted of the psychosocial development stages by Erik Erikson with the focus being placed on the adolescent stage of development. This model of development suggests that there are eight stages as an individual transitions through his or her life. The fourth stage, the adolescent stage, is defined as *identity versus role confusion* (Erikson 1968). This stage involves people either establishing a clear understanding of their identities and the roles they are to portray, or—if they do not successfully complete the stage—they are left in crisis, which results in role confusion (Crawford et al. 2004;). Erikson's theory contends that successful completion of the adolescent stage results in positive role identity; however, development of a positive role identity is equivalent to a positive sense of self-worth. The sense of self-worth is a continuous behavior that leads to the next stage of Erikson's psychosocial development model, *intimacy formation*. Erikson describes intimacy formation as a time in which individuals shares themselves with others while maintaining their own identities.

Mercer (2004) found that achievement of maternal identity occurs once the mother has intimate knowledge of her infant and feels competent and confident in her parenting. Mercer contended in additional research that the maternal identity was based on her previous work of mother role attainment theory, which she has replaced with the new term *BAM* (Mercer 2004). It is also anticipated that there is a difference between younger and older mothers with regard to self-concept, parenting skills, and attitudes about parenting. The differences all involve the varying effects of the interruption of the adolescent time period on the adolescent mother.

It was also anticipated that the interruption of adolescence due to pregnancy would have a greater effect on the younger adolescent mother's transition into motherhood because of her not completing the adolescent developmental stage.

Organization of the Remainder of the Study

Understanding the phenomena of an adolescent mother's transition to developing her maternal-role identity, the psychosocial development processes, and the influential elements of a teen mother's parenting attitudes were essential elements to the study. Chapter 2 provides a comprehensive review of past and current empirical research on the dynamics of teen childbearing, adolescent parenting, urban living, and the transition into motherhood. Chapter 3 describes the groundwork of the phenomenological research methods and research design. Chapter 4 provides the results from the research, and chapter 5 discusses the results and conclusions.

Chapter 2

REVIEW OF LITERATURE

This study identified the experiences of urban adolescent mothers regarding their perceptions, thoughts, and feelings related to their transition to motherhood from adolescence. The qualitative research study gathered information to develop an understanding of how urban adolescent mothers transition to their role of becoming a mother and to identify the psychosocial impact that early childbearing has on overall maternal identity development. The transitional phenomenon of urban young mothers' transformation from adolescents to young mothers was explored through the use of the phenomenological research design and in-depth, face-to-face interviews with urban adolescent mothers between the ages of eighteen and twenty-two. For the purpose of this study, the terms *adolescent mother, teen mother, and young mother* are all used interchangeably. They are defined as a woman at the onset of puberty, is between the ages of ten and twenty-three, and who gave birth to a child and assumed the role of a mother (Borkowski, Whitman, and Farris 2007).

This chapter provides an overview of the research and literature with regard to the culture of urban adolescent motherhood—as well as the cognitive and emotional factors associated with this population. The literature review also includes themes relating to urban adolescent mothers and their experiences as they transcend into motherhood. The literature review describes theories used to assist in the explanation of the precipitating phenomenon: Erikson's

(1968) psychosocial development theory; Mercer's (2004) BAM theory, and Kaiser and Hays's (2004) conceptual model. In addition to the three theoretical frameworks addressed in the literature review, four themes resonating throughout the literature are (a) adolescent mothers experiencing high levels of stress and anxiety at the onset of their becoming mothers, (b) ecological factors playing a major role in the lives of urban adolescent mothers (e.g., emotional and financial factors), (c) parenting stressors having a drastic effect on young mothers and their children's well-being, and (d) adolescent mothers struggling with the duality of being a teen and becoming a mother. The identified themes guided and supported the research topic and provided additional details regarding the urban adolescents' transition to motherhood.

Current Status of Teenage Pregnancy

For the past twenty years, more attention has been given to the culture of teen pregnancy because of the inverted outcomes that often result from early childbearing (Furstenberg et al. 1987; Hamilton, Martin, and Ventura 2012; Hurlburt and McDonald 1997; Lipman et al. 2011). Numerous studies have been conducted outlining the effects of early childbearing on our economy from federal, state, and local perspectives (Meadows–Oliver et al. 2007; Sangalang 2006; SmithBattle and Leonard 2012). This section addresses the current statistics and risk factors and provides a historical overview of teen pregnancy and the results of early childbearing.

Current Statistics

Compared with other industrialized western nations, the United States has the highest rates of teen pregnancy, teen birth, STDs, and abortion (Singh and Darroch 2000). In 2011, 329,797 babies were born to US women between the ages of fifteen and nineteen years, accounting for a live birth rate of 31.3 per thousand women in this age group, according to the Centers for Disease Control and

Prevention (CDC; Hamilton et al. 2012). In that age group, there was a record low for US teen births and a drop of 8 percent from 2010 results. The birth rates for teens aged fifteen to seventeen fell 11 percent, and for teens aged eighteen to nineteen it fell 7 percent (Martinez, Copen, and Abma 2011). Minority youth (such as African Americans, Hispanics/Latinas, and Native Americans) who are socioeconomically disadvantaged continue to have the highest rates of teen pregnancy and early childbirth; these ethnic groups comprised 57 percent of US teen births in 2011 (Hamilton et al. 2012). The CDC has documented that teen pregnancy also highly affects youth in the foster care and juvenile justice systems.

Teen pregnancy and childbirth results in nearly $11 billion per year in costs to US taxpayers for increased services (including healthcare and foster care), increased incarceration rates among children of teen parents, and lost tax revenue because of lower educational attainment and income among teen mothers (National Campaign to Prevent Teen and Unplanned Pregnancy 2010, 2014). A primary factor for high school dropout rates for women is pregnancy and birth (Perper, Peterson, and Manlove 2010). By the age of twenty-two, only 50 percent of teen mothers received a high school diploma—compared with 90 percent of women who did not give birth during adolescence (Perper et al. 2010).

Early childbearing not only affects the mother by increasing her likelihood of unemployment as an adult, but also it can have negative consequences for the children of teenage mothers (Hoffman and Maynard 2008; Whitman et al. 2001). Children of teenage mothers have been found to have a higher chance of dropping out of school, lower academic success, increased health problems, and more engagements with the juvenile justice system during their adolescence; they are also more likely to experience teen pregnancy themselves (Hoffman and Maynard 2008). The dismal outcomes often affect teen mothers who are already socioeconomically disadvantaged. Some live in communities plagued with violence and drugs and have minimal educational aspiration; early childbirth often makes successful outcomes even harder to achieve without considering the numerous risk factors that affect the possibilities of success (Hoffman and Maynard 2008; Singh and Darroch 2000).

Risk Factors Associated With Early Childbearing

Teen childbearing causes various outcomes, ranging from creating positive changes and outlooks on the young mother's life (Shanok and Miller 2007a) to negative consequences that include increased depression (Edwards et al. 2012), increased risk of poverty (Oxford, Lee, and Lohr 2010), interruption of education (Noria et al. 2007), and poor parenting practices (Alan Guttmacher Institute 2004). This section provides an overview of the documented studies and research pertaining to the most prevalent effects of early childbearing.

The research is inundated with empirical evidence that identifies the circumstances and consequences of early childbearing (Brien and Willis 1997; Coley and Chase-Lansdale 1998; Furstenberg et al. 1987; Geronimus and Korenman 1992; Hoffman and Maynard 1997; Whitman et al. 2001). In addition to the risk associated with early childbearing, studies have identified the resilient factors young mothers use to overcome the trials and tribulations often associated with early childbearing (Furstenberg et al. 1987; Wright and Davis 2008). Early childbearing is often the precursor to environmental and social risk factors that have caused many speculations for the increasing number of childbearing teens in the United States, especially those in inner cities (Hard et al. 1997; Turley 2003).

The common risk factors include poverty, certain racial and ethnic backgrounds, mental health status, and low self-concept (Driscoll et al. 2005; Henretta 2007; Taylor 2010). In addition, teenagers who live in areas with signs of poverty (such as high crime rate, single-parent families, and lower levels of education among residents) are at the highest risk for teenage pregnancy (Yampolskaya, Brown, and Vargo 2004).

The National Campaign to Prevent Teen and Unplanned Pregnancy associated teenage childbearing with negative consequences and outcomes for the teen mother, her child, and their family (2006, 2010, 2014). The campaign also found that teens most likely to become pregnant are already at risk and affected by the economic strains of living in poverty—which accounts for the lack of resources and social supports—as well as the overall disadvantages of oppression and inequalities. Most teen pregnancies tend to have a negative impact on both the mother and child because of the lack of basic resources and the need to depend on others for daily necessities such as health care, transportation, and daycare (Terry-Humen, Manlove, and Cottingham 2006). Teen pregnancy and motherhood not only directly impact the teen mother's social mobility and chance of completing school, but also they have a direct effect on her family and her child. Unfortunately, teen mothers residing in urban areas must deal with issues of motherhood while dealing with the effects of urban living—such as crime, poverty, and a lack of resources (Eshbaugh, Lempers, and Luze 2006). Many of the mothers lack the basic knowledge of child development, and few have the skills and patience to deal with many stresses of motherhood. Teens are still in the process of developing their own identities and attempting to understand their roles as both mothers and as teenagers (Eshbaugh et al. 2006).

Historical Frameworks of Adolescent Motherhood

Adolescent motherhood has been examined in the past in light of the negative effects of early childbearing (Brien and Willis 1997; Coley and Chase-Lansdale 1998; Furstenberg et al. 1987; Geronimus and Korenman 1992; Hoffman and Maynard 1997; Whitman et al. 2001). However, in the past, teenage motherhood was viewed as "unwed mothering," which was also often viewed as a detrimental element with negative impacts on a child's life. All too often, previous research highlighted poverty, lack of education, criminal involvement, and children with behavioral problems. Furstenberg et al. (1987) conducted a landmark longitudinal study on urban adolescent mothers and their children. The widely cited research continues to be relevant. The results of the study have provided more positive insight on the effects of early childbearing and have introduced additional parameters in which the culture of teen mothering can be addressed.

Furstenberg et al. (1987) examined the fate of adolescent children from childhood through adolescence. The mothers were recruited to participate in what was known as the "Baltimore Project," which began in Baltimore, Maryland in 1966. The adolescent mothers who participated in this study yielded varying outcomes after the seventeen-year longitudinal follow-up, which tracked their transition from adolescents into parenthood.

The study examined maternal outcomes such as income level, welfare status, and the number of subsequent children. Results revealed that the mothers who had moderate incomes—compared with the working poor or welfare recipients—were economically sound and secure, resulting in fewer childbirths. A key marker of developing a long-term welfare status was the education level of the grandparents, which was independent of the teen mother's own educational status. Furstenberg et al. concluded that grandparents with more education had greater economic and social resources to assist their teen granddaughters in becoming independent and being effective parents. Finally, the strongest predictor of fertility was the length of time before the secondary pregnancy. Furstenberg et al. found that delaying the subsequent pregnancy was a stronger indicator for limiting the total number of pregnancies. This factor could be attributed to the participation in school and community intervention programs, which also suggested that the availability of resources and supportive services might have compensated for the lack of familial and personal resources. The seventeen-year follow up revealed that 296 adolescent children of teenage mothers exhibited "massive school failure," with half having to repeat a grade level along with 61 percent professing they were C or D students (Furstenberg et al. 2007, 148).

The subsequent thirty-year follow up using the data from the same cohort found that maternal determining factors—such as marital status and the number of years spent on public assistance—had a direct influence on the youths' educational and economic success (Furstenberg, Furstenberg, and Hughes 1993). Furstenberg's 1993 study also found many factors exposing the teen mothers to early poverty, causing them to struggle with managing their transition from the adolescent stage to parenthood. Furstenberg et al. found that more than 60 percent of the youth born to teen mothers compellingly overcame the challenges and disadvantages their teen mothers had faced.

In 2007, Furstenberg conducted a thirty-year follow up of his study and found that early childbearing is neither a permanent nor long-term cause of poverty. Furstenberg also found that over the course of time, teen mothers were able to sustain marriage and employment and eventually complete their education, including higher education. Within the first seventeen years of the study, the teen mother participants lives begun to stabilize and their lives became aligned with their their peers who delayed pregnancy within five years of childbirth. Therefore, Furstenberg (2007) concluded that there were noted improvements in the seventeen- and thirty-year studies; however, many of the improvements began before the seventeen-year study.

A second longitudinal study was conducted during the same time as the Baltimore Project; this study was conducted in New Haven, Connecticut by Horwitz et al. (1991). Horwitz et al. also examined teen mothers living in an urban area. The twenty-year follow-up data from the study yielded similar results, which supported the Baltimore Project's general findings. The study found that 66 percent of the teen mothers had completed high school, the majority had recently been on welfare, and most had more than one—but fewer than four—children (Horwitz et al. 1991). The longitudinal study revealed that becoming a teen mother presents difficulties; however, overcoming the obstacles is a possibility with viable resources, willingness to succeed, and a strong support system.

A longitudinal study conducted in 1984 by the Notre Dame Adolescent Parenting Project (NDAPP) examined the psychological and social consequences of teen parenting on mothers and their children.

The study was conducted in four phases over twenty years. The first two phases revealed that during pregnancy, adolescent mothers experienced social, emotional, and behavioral problems. They experienced problems with support and feelings of being less prepared for parenting. During years three, five, and eight, and after the birth of the first baby, the mothers tended to be undereducated, underemployed, and to continue to give birth to additional children. A high level of instability in the maternal functioning was also noted over time, which appeared to be associated with personal adjustment. Six months after giving birth to their first child, the mothers displayed minimal knowledge about parenting and children, high levels of stress, and problematic parenting styles (Whitman et al. 2001). Many of the mothers were at risk of neglectful and abusive parenting because of their inadequate readiness to parent (Borkowski, Whitman, and Farris 2007). The study also found when the children were around eight years old, 38 percent of the mothers were depressed. More specifically, mild, moderate, and severe depression were observed in 20.85 percent, 11.7 percent, and 5.2 percent of the sample, respectively. Early parenting brought on increasingly large amounts of stress and unexpected conflicts between the young mother's need to nurture her child along with her own need for nurturance. The unmet need of nurturance in the young mother often resulted in elevated levels of stress and anxiety, which in turn led to abusive and neglectful parenting practices (Borkowski, Whitman, and Farris 2007). The young mothers' interactions with their children and tolerance levels were observed; they were found to be more intolerant, more impatient, more insensitive, more punitive, and less accessible and verbal compared with adult mothers (Borkowoski, Whitman, and Farris 2007).

The overall parenting styles of young mothers during the NDAPP study was later linked to developmental delays in their children (Whitman et al. 2001). Finally, the eight-year assessment revealed that more than half of the mothers (53.6 percent) reported currently being employed, and 28 percent reported being enrolled in and attending school at least on a part-time basis.

The average number of years of education received was 11.9, and at least 82.3 percent had a desire to or planned to go back to finish school. The researchers found that the most frequently cited obstacles for the mothers' continuing education were the costs of tuition and childcare (Borkowoski, Whitman, and Farris 2007).

The longitudinal study yielded similar results regarding the overall long-term effects of early childbearing among teen mothers. Significant findings on the emotional and psychological effects of stress and anxiety on the young mother have been found to directly affect her parenting and also affect the development of her child (Borkowski, Whitman, and Farris 2007). Repeat pregnancies were noted as a significant factor directly affecting the teen mother's ability to successfully progress past the initial hurdles and obstacles teen mothers endure (Noria et al. 2007; Furstenberg et al. 1987, 1993; Horwitz et al. 1991). Finally, studies also verify that adolescent mothers experience multiple challenges as they transition into their roles of motherhood.

Adolescent motherhood is not a one-dimensional phenomenon; it incorporates emotional, psychological, and social factors that affect parenting outcomes (Postmus, Huang, and Mathisen-Stylianou 2012; SmithBattle and Leonard 2012). In addition to the emotional and physical hurdles experienced by adolescent mothers, Hurbult and McDonald (1997) studied the psychosocial effects of early childbearing on adolescent mothers. They investigated the developmental and transitional factors that adolescent mothers experience as they transitioned to motherhood. Hurlburt and McDonald (1997) investigated how psychosocial elements of development (such as self-esteem) had a direct impact on the parenting knowledge of adolescent mothers. Using Erikson's psychosocial development theory, they found significant correlations between the adolescent mother's parenting knowledge—as it related to her understanding her role, empathy, the use of corporal punishment, and the developmental expectations of her child—and her self-esteem. Data from this study supported the notion that adolescent self-esteem is developmentally continuous (Hurlburt and McDonald 1997). The study also implied a correlation between appropriate knowledge of role reversal and self-esteem. The work of Hurlburt and McDonald supported the work of Hubbs-Tait (1986), which asserted that adolescent parenting practices could be understood as an element of an adolescent stage of development (Hurlburt and McDonald 1997). The results of their research supported the notion that if the adolescent mother has not developed her role identity, she can be at risk for poor parenting practices. According to Erikson's psychosocial development theory, a role identity must be established to parent, as this is a perquisite to the generativity stage of development.

Ecological Factors of Adolescent Motherhood

Motherhood involves many ecological elements that have a direct effect on mothers and their children (Corcoran, Franklin, and Bennett 2000; Levine, Emery, and Pollack 2007). Lipman et al. (2011) found that children born to teen mothers versus nonteen mothers were associated with poorer educational achievement, lower life satisfaction, and less personal income. They also suggested in their study that children of teen mothers had an increased chance of being exposed to family-related socioeconomic disadvantages, as did mothers with mental health issues and lower levels of education. Previous research (Brien and Willis 1997; Coley and Chase-Lansdale, 1998; Furstenberg 1987; Whitman et al. 2001) has documented the negative outcomes caused by negative ecological factors associated with early childbearing (Levine et al. 2007). For example, the lack of educational attainment has a direct impact on a mother's educational and financial potential. The lack of financial stability and the perception of no plausible positive solutions result in increased mental health disparities and possible self-medicating treatments such as alcohol, substance abuse, violence, and other destructive coping mechanisms (Bartlett and Easterbrooks 2012). Finally, being predisposed to environmental factors such as poverty, high crime, and violence often exacerbates the problems of early childbearing because it adds additional stressors to a convoluted situation (Lipman et al. 2011; Postmus et al. 2012).

Postmus et al. (2012) described ecological factors associated with outcomes on mothers' mental health and parenting, particularly those related to financial, physical, and psychological abuse. The study also indicated relationships between specified types of abuse (such as physical, psychological, or economic) and maternal outcomes, including depression and parenting problems (failure to engage with child or spanking the child). In year one of the study, mothers who had experienced physical, psychological, or economic abuse were likely to have expressive-depressive episodes in year five. The study also revealed how different types of abuse affected the lack of maternal engagement with the child and the use of spanking as discipline. Results indicated that the mothers who were exposed to economic or psychological abuse were less likely to engage in parent-child activities and more likely to use spanking as a form of discipline. The lack of financial instability was linked to spanking. Researchers concluded that the lack of control and power over finances—and not having sound means to improve or provide financial security through work or school—potentially may leave mothers feeling hopeless and powerless, which may make them resort to spanking as a disciplinary tactic.

Varying ecological components have been shown to have a direct impact on early childbearing, and often cases of predisposed intergenerational elements affect parenting (Corcoran et al. 2000; Meade, Kershaw and Ickovics 2008). The ecological elements include environmental, cultural, and emotional elements (Lewin et al. 2011). In this section of the literature review, specific ecological factors were highlighted, including urban living, the cultural components of how adolescent mothers cope with their role as mothers, and the psychosocial and emotional factors that affect their transition to motherhood.

Environmental Factors of Urban Living

High crime and violence are well-documented elements of urban living (Lewin et al. 2011). Previous research conducted on minority children growing up in urban environments—where they are constantly exposed to violence—examined the impact of violence. Exposure to violence has been found to have a direct impact on academic achievement, behaviors, and levels of posttraumatic stress (Brockenbrough, Cornell, and Loper 2002; Postmus et al. 2012; Thompson and Massat 2005). Living in urban environments has also been linked to high levels of teenage pregnancy and violent partnerships.

Thompson and Massat (2005) studied the effect of witnessing violence in the family in a community of 110 African American children in Chicago, Illinois. Results revealed that levels of family exposure to violence had a significant effect on related behavior problems and a negative effect on academic achievement in school. In addition, Thompson and Massat found that exposure to community violence was associated with behavioral problems and academic achievement. Academic achievement was not related to behavior, however; it was significantly related to symptomologies associated with PTSD in relation to the exposure of family and community to the violence. PTSD has varying effects on adolescents, children, and teenagers. In the study, adolescents and teenagers responded to PTSD as adults and had a period of *posttraumatic acting out*. The study also indicated prevalent behaviors displayed by teenagers who were exposed to violence—including delinquency and school truancy, precocious sexual activity, and substance abuse (Eth and Pynoos 1994; Thompson and Massat 2006).

Kennedy and Bennett (2006) contended that African American or Latina urban adolescent mothers were more vulnerable to exposure to violence and were generally poor or low income. Interpersonal violence was found to be significantly linked to adolescent mothers who had endured or experienced community violence (Kennedy 2006). Research also shows not only that adolescent girls are vulnerable to the distress associated with exposure to violence, but also that there are intergenerational implications for adolescent mothers (Aisenberg and Ell 2005; Kennedy 2006). An emerging social issue among poor African American women between ages sixteen and twenty-four is high levels of partner violence (Kennedy 2006). Furthermore, 34–65 percent of the women receiving public assistance—and those who had their first children when they were adolescents— reported having higher rates of partner violence (Kennedy 2006).

Finally, adolescent mothers who reported a history of physical abuse by a parent or caregiver and reported that they had been sexually abused—or had experienced partner violence—were found to have higher school dropout rates, higher stress, more depression, and increased substance abuse during pregnancy (Kennedy and Bennett 2006).

Research suggests adolescents residing in urban areas plagued with crime and violence endure a great deal of exposure to violence through psychological, community, and relational forces (Kennedy 2006; Kreager, Matsueda, and Erosheva 2010; Taylor 2010). Increased exposure to violence serves as an additional road block to the adolescent mother to achieving success. A solution that resonated in research conducted on urban living, community violence, and partner violence was the use of social support to assist adolescent mothers to manage the dilemmas associated with urban living and exposure to violence (Harrykissoon, Rickert, and Wiemann 2002; Lesser and Koniak-Griffin 2000).

Emotional Factors Associated with the Transition To Motherhood

Adolescent mothers endure the interruption of their teen life and take on the responsibilities and duties associated with adult parenthood. The emotional factors associated with the development of this dual identity have been analyzed in the literature. Adolescent mothers find their new roles as parents often grueling, requiring them to endure high amounts of stress and experience emotional–social maladjustments (Logsdon et al. 2008). The psychosocial adjustments endured by teen mothers once they give birth include various clinical diagnoses, such as depression (Knoche et al. 2007). Early childbearing in adolescents also contributes to the onset of additional relational and personal parenting issues, including lack of resources and support, mental and physical exhaustion, and social isolation from family and friends (Birkeland et al. 2005).

Zimmer et al. (2001) studied the psychosocial outcome of adolescents born to teen mothers. Findings suggested that social structures that determine health and adolescent development were problematic; this was a more informative approach than solely examining the effects of the mother's age. This point is further explained in a study conducted by Drummond et al. (2008). They found that adolescent mothers have more unrealistic expectations from their child's behavior and are less verbal and less responsive to their infants. They were also found to lack patience and to be more prone to use corporal punishment as a form of discipline.

Drummond et al. concluded that adolescent mothers often struggle with social stressors. Stressors are a normal part of adolescence, but these are in addition to the stressors of transitioning to parenthood. The personal stressors, parental stressors, and the lack of maturity of adolescent mothers are likely to interfere with their ability to respond to their infants' cues (Drummond et al. 2008).

Theoretical Models and Frameworks

Erikson's Adolescent Stage Development

Erik Erikson's psychosocial development theory asserts that human life progresses through eight fixed stages. The ages of the stages vary according to the individual; however, each stage must be endured and experienced before moving on to the subsequent stage (Erikson 1968). Erikson noted that each stage is marked by either a *crisis* when one does not complete the stage or a "necessary turning point, a crucial moment, when development must move one way or another, marshaling resources of growth, recovery, and further differentiation" (Erikson, 1968), which must be resolved before growth can occur. The process of the stages concludes with the premise that any unresolved stage leaves the individual in a state of "crisis," which hinders the development of all succeeding stages (Erikson 1968). However, if the individual experiences conflict and finds resolution in the earlier stages of development, the method of resolution influences the conflict resolution in subsequent stages.

Adolescence is a time when an individual builds self-reliance and seeks independence but also requires assistance and guidance to understand and evaluate the ambivalence that intercedes with daily life. Adolescent mothers often struggle with completing the developmental task of the adolescent stage. According to Erikson's psychosocial development theory, the struggle to complete the adolescent stage is caused by the conflicting task of identity and role confusion achievement. Both of these directly affect the adolescent mother simultaneously, leaving her in the psychological paradox of being an adolescent and also being a parent (Hurlburt and McDonald 1997; Kaye 2008; 1997; Zastrow and Kirst-Ashman 2006).

According to Erikson (1968), a key element to adolescent transition is exploration. Erikson asserted that identity crisis takes place through exploration, and the crisis does not have to be acute or severe in nature. Erikson characterized adolescent identity exploration as being a part of ego strength; cognitive restructuring and the view of self are often the result of reduced ego strength and an impairment of coping (Kidwell et al. 1995). The adolescent transition is also marked by symptoms that include acting out, confusion, ego defense, impulsivity, mood swings, heightened physical and somatic complaints, and subjective discomfort (Erikson 1968; Kidwell et al. 1995). Erikson also asserted that during self in transition an adolescent is vulnerable due to their incipient growth and awareness. Each stage becomes a crisis, which plays a significant part in the functions that mesh together with the shift of the instinctual energy and the specific vulnerable part (Erikson 1959, 56). Under these challenges of vulnerable moments, the experience is what Erikson's calls a *split of images*, which is a loss of one's center and process dispersion (Erikson 1968).

Erikson described the experience of identity formation as the dark and negative side of development and viewed this as an intricate part of the identity process. The identity versus role confusion stage shows there is a developmental need for the self to establish identity during the adolescent phase. Identity versus role confusion is also useful in examining the transition from childhood to adulthood and the formulation of roles and perceptions of self. There is an essential need for adolescents to achieve an identity during that adolescent phase. Erikson found that identity is necessary to progress to the next stage of development and to be prepared to make imperative decisions and build self-esteem (Erikson 1968).

During the adolescent stage of development, the young mother is known to abandon her psychological search for identity and prematurely begin to take on the role of adulthood. Adolescent mothers skip through the intimacy versus isolation stage, which is when they would generally experience and learn "I am what I love." According to Erikson, adolescent mothers don't learn to relate their deepest hopes and fears to other individuals or to accept others' intimacy in return (Erikson 1968). In sharing intimacy, an individual builds self-confidence and security.

Therefore, when adolescent mothers are thrust into the stage of adulthood, they give up their social experimentation, which is normally accepted during adolescence (Erikson 1968). The goal of adulthood is to accomplish generativity, which in essence provides resolution to the issue of I am what I care for. This situation causes a psychological paradox, because the adolescent neglects to find the answer to Who am I? before I am what I care for because of the interruption of the adolescent stage and being thrust into adulthood.

In his description of his psychosocial stages, Erikson (1968) noted there are often reciprocal effects among the various domains of the developmental stages. He asserted that conflicts often arise from societal expectations imposed on individuals as their interpersonal spectra widen to include the physical maturation that occurs simultaneously. During the adolescent stage, the various developmental tasks emerge as the ego focuses on mastering the environment. It has also been found that the developmental tasks are never completely finished; however, they can be renegotiated later in life with the introduction of new experiences (Boyce 1988).

Mercer's Becoming a Mother (BAM) Theory

Mercer (1985) found very few studies at the time focused on the mother's perception of competence and role efficacy. The findings from these studies (when compared with perceptions of competency and efficacy among twenty- and thirty-year-old mothers) showed the importance of these factors in shaping the experience of motherhood (Mercer 1986). The multiple experiences endured in the motherhood process lead to the development and establishment of maternal identity. The new mother evolves into her role, defining her new self and her commitment (Mercer 2004).

Mercer (2004) found there was more to maternal role attainment than identity development. With validation from numerous qualitative studies on maternal-role identity and development, Mercer (2004) decided to discontinue using the terms *maternal role attainment* and to instead use the term *BAM* (for *becoming a mother*).

Maternal identity contributes to the psychosocial development in becoming a mother (Mercer 2004). The overall process of this development includes continual change and a period of transition before transformation. The transitions incorporate varying cognitive, physical, and social elements, all of which directly affect the mother's process of "becoming a mother." Cultural beliefs, attitudes, socioeconomic status, community and societal conditions, and preparation and knowledge all are elements included in the transitional process (Mercer 2004).

According to Nelson (2003), the process of transformation occurs when the mother begins with the expansion of self, widening the scope of capabilities, redefining self and relationships, and incorporating motherhood into her sense of self.

Nelson also identified motherhood as a process of primary engagement in a study that reviewed motherhood in North America and Australia. The primary engagement process was defined as a commitment—becoming engrossed and actively involved with the child's presence as well as providing care for the child.

Mercer (2006) also asserted that the process of becoming a mother requires extensive psychological, social, and physical work from the mother. Mercer found women often experience a heightened level of vulnerability and face challenges as they make the transition to being a mother. The BAM process entails the influences of the mother, friends, community, and societal environments, which all assist her in transitioning into her new role.

Mercer identified empathetic listening and interactive dialogue with the mother and her influencers as important approaches to assist her with her transition.

BAM largely encompasses the concept of maternal identity as a component of meeting its goals. However, the mother's maternal identity continuously morphs as she meets new challenges and experiences in her new motherhood process (Mercer 2004). During this process, she is able to explore and gain self-confidence in her role as a mother (Mercer 2004). Mercer named four stages in the process of maternal identity BAM: (a) commitment, attachment, and preparation (pregnancy), (b) acquaintance, learning, and physical restoration to a new normal (two to six weeks), (c) moving toward a new normal (two weeks to four months), and (d) achievement of the maternal identity (around four months). The times for the stages fluctuate and are influenced by maternal and infant variables as well as the social environment. The stages also overlap and are continuous depending on what the mother is enduring at the time of her maternal identity process.

The commitment, attachment, and preparation stage has long-range implications as the mother is actively involved with becoming acclimated and adapted to motherhood. In the acquaintance, learning, and physical restoration stage, the mother becomes familiar with her baby and learns techniques such as soothing and calming him or her.

She also studies her baby for resemblance to family members, wholeness, and functioning of body parts. Moving toward a new normal involves the mother structuring her mothering to fit her new lifestyle. She makes adjustments to the changed relationships with partners, family, and friends as she attempts to settle into her new self. Here is where a great deal of cognitive restricting begins to take place as she learns her baby's cues and adjusts to her new reality.

Achieving maternal identity requires an intimate knowledge of herself and her infant to the point where she is confident in herself and her skills as a mother. She will settle into herself and her new role, and she will establish a new normal with her relationships with her family. A transformation of self will occur along with her transformation as a mother as she expands herself to infuse her new identity. She will assume her responsibility of taking care of her infant along with setting goals for herself and her infant in the future (Mercer 2004).

Kaiser and Hays's Psychosocial Adjustment and Conceptual Model

The conceptual model from Kaiser and Hays (2004) emphasizes the fact that pregnancy and the adolescent stage of development represent *dual developmentalism*—two developmental tasks working simultaneously. Kaiser and Hays developed the APQ, which assesses the transition to motherhood and the influence of psychosocial factors on the transitional process. The four psychosocial factors are accepting the pregnancy, planning for the future, viewing self as a mother, and growing up. Kaiser and Hays found that these factors may positively or negatively affect the transition into motherhood. Those four concepts will be used to identity their effect on the adolescent mother's transition.

The conceptual model reviews the developmental tasks that adolescent mothers undertake as adolescents and the developmental task of becoming a mother. The dual developmentalism is a process Kaiser and Hays (2004) described as a including developing as an adolescent and becoming a mother simultaneously.

The success of the transition to motherhood is heavily influenced by psychosocial factors, and the successful completion of the transition depends on the process in which the developmental task occurs (Kaiser and Hays 2004). The APQ is a tool used to identify the psychosocial factors that influence the young mother's thoughts and behaviors. Being able to identify their influences enables health practitioners and others to assist the young mothers. It can help in prevention and intervention to eliminate the high risk of postpartum depression and other emotional and physical risks that young mothers often endure (Kaiser and Hays 2004).

The elements of the APQ are key factors to be aware of when interviewing young mothers; they may help identify some of the factors that had an influence on the mothers while they were pregnant and during postpartum.

Teen mothers are emotional beings. In previous qualitative studies, the participants often mentioned their feelings and emotions once they found out they were pregnant and after having the baby (Kaiser and Hays 2004). As noted by Kaiser and Hays, the four psychosocial factors may positively or negatively influence the transitions to motherhood in the following ways: (a) accepting the pregnancy was important, because poor acceptance can lead to disequilibrium and can cause conflict, which can affect the teen's perception of the level of support from the family, (b) adjustment in the teen's awareness of the need to grow up or begin to develop a sense of responsibility may influence the teen's understanding of what to expect during pregnancy and the transition into motherhood, (c) plans for the future may be altered because of pregnancy, and previous goals and aspirations will be adjusted to include the baby in the life trajectory, and (d) finally, having a lack of awareness is signified when a mother has difficulty viewing herself as a mother. This lack of awareness creates role conflict and affects the emotional well-being of the mother if she has an impairment during development of the maternal identity (Kaiser and Hays 2004; Mercer 2004).

Transition From Teenager to Adolescent Mother to Parenthood

The research often provides a framework for adolescent mothers with respect to their immaturity and "lack of readiness" to parent (Lashley, Hans, and Henson 2009). *Readiness* in the literature is often operationally defined in terms of child development awareness and knowledge as they relate to the level of parenting, as well as in terms of adolescent mothers' levels of socioemotional or cognitive development (Whitman et al. 2001). In addressing the issue of parenting readiness and level of cognitive maturity to parent, previous research often lacked the explanations of the transitional process that adolescent mothers endure as they begin to mature and establish adequate parenting skills to effectively parent their babies. Lashley et al. found that parenting development occurs during a mother's transition into motherhood, which is embedded in the relationship established between mother and baby.

Motherhood is perceived as one of the identifiable developmental markers that leads to adulthood. Flanagan et al. (1995) described it as the "interpersonal reorganization" that occurs in the transition from *nonparent* to *parent*. However, the transition of becoming a mother can be cumbersome and convoluted for young mothers who endure or understand their roles when they are integrated with the developmental task of adolescence (Booth, Rustenbach, and McHale 2008; Flanagan et al. 1995; Hanna 2001; Larson 2004; Oxford et al. 2010). During the process of becoming a parent, adolescent mothers battle with both cognitive and psychosocial developmental tasks of identity awareness (Flanagan 1995) and development.

These tasks can cause the adolescent to endure a psychological crisis (Noria et al. 2007), which inadvertently affects her transition process of becoming a mother and parenting. This section discusses the transition process of adolescent mothers and the intricate transformations they undergo.

The process of transitioning from adolescence to adult parenthood is an ongoing psychological battle filled with personal exploration, social negotiations, and fluctuating emotions (Barratt et al. 1996; Hurlburt and McDonald 1997; Kaye 2008; Noria et al. 2007).

Adolescence is a time for egocentric ideologies, concentration on self, dependence on family, and evolution of identity (Steinberg and Morris 2001). After the adolescent phase is complete, the emergence of the young adulthood phase ideally occurs between the ages of eighteen and twenty-five. This time period has been described as the identity exploration in the context of worldviews, love, and working with others (Booth et al. 2008). Ideally, young people delay the undertaking of adult-simulated roles such as parenting and taking care of a family.

Identity development is a marker that includes increased autonomy, a progression of independence from the family, and increased social interactions with peers (Erikson 1968). The irony of identity development for adolescent mothers is the presence of conflicting roles of being an adolescent while also being a "responsible parenting adult." They develop their own sense of self and their own maternal-role identity as well as developing their adult-role responsibilities. Adolescent mothers engage in dueling identity development during their transition to parenthood, self-identity, and maternal identity (Merriwether-de Vries 2000). According to Erikson's psychosocial development theory, the unsuccessful completion or resolution of the adolescence stage contributes to difficulties in future transitions and phases in life (Erikson 1968; Marcia 1976).

When early childbearing occurs, the mother is forced into an incomplete phase of autonomy that includes adult duties and responsibilities. *Autonomy* refers to the adolescent's emergence into independence. This emergence is achieved through adaptive behaviors learned through school, employment, or relationships; maladaptive independence is achieved through risky behaviors (Oberlander et al. 2009). The term *relatedness* refers to maintaining a positive reciprocal relationship with parents in which the socialization process and family values are learned. Researchers felt relatedness was very important to minority adolescents because of the strong cultural values taught and the potential of relatedness to provide protection from daily stressors (Chang and Fine 2007; Fouquier 2011; Oberlander et al. 2009; Taylor 2010). Burton (2007) described the *adultification* process that occurs in the absence of secure parental attachment as children in low-income families take on adult roles and responsibilities, such as childbearing. Expanding on Burton's work, Sangalang, Barth, and Painter (2006) examined a case management intervention program for first-time teen mothers and parenting adolescents. They found that African American teen mothers have an increased risk of having inadequate prenatal care, low birth weight for their babies, and preterm births. In addition, they found that young maternal age, race, marital status, and smoking were the predictors for poor prenatal care and birth outcomes, along with the likelihood of subsequent births. Their study recommended that providing adequate support and intervention to teen mothers past their high school years would be beneficial during these emerging adulthood years. They also suggested practitioners engage with this population to examine the needs of the mothers and address the challenges they often face during this period (Burton 2007; Sangalang et al. 2006).

Oberlander et al. (2009) contended that the simultaneous existence of both autonomy and the relatedness process leads to ego development, high self-esteem development, and precursors for a healthy transition into adulthood. However, early childbearing disrupts this developmental process of adolescence, which often alters the progression of a successful autonomy and relatedness process. The disruption tends to leave adolescent mothers ill-prepared and lacking the necessary resources needed for parenthood, which results in a high reliance on their family for support (Salder and Cowlin 2003).

Adolescent mothers often experience turbulence as they transition to taking on the duties and roles of being a mother (Brubaker and Wright 2006; Flanagan et al. 1995; Kaiser and Hays 2004). Only minimal research captures the elements of the experience as teen mothers transition from a cognitive, emotional, or behavioral basis—without the research being coated with negative outcomes and overtones. Various themes evolved from qualitative studies conducted on adolescent mothers; however, a large portion of them has concentrated on pregnant teens and new adolescent mothers. In a mixed-method study exploring the transitions to motherhood by inner-city, pregnant and newly parenting teens, Shanok and Miller (2007b) found that although few teens planned to have a baby, a large percentage of the 80 participants were pleased to discover their pregnancy. A heightened sense of purpose emerged, and the expectant mothers developed drastically increased safety conscious behaviors. The teens also sometimes experienced periods of public and familial alienation. Shanok and Miller (2007a) found teenage mothers reported increased motivation to complete school and a heightened sense of maturity and responsibility.

Similar tales of triumph resonate in the literature. Teen mothers have stated that having a child motivated them to stay in school, work harder, disassociate themselves from criminal activities (such as gangs and drugs), and reestablish broken relationships with family members (Furstenberg 2007; Jacobs and Mollborn 2012; Lesser et al. 2003; Shanok and Miller 2007a; Wright and Davis 2008). In their study of 162 disadvantaged, urban, single mothers in Philadelphia, Pennsylvania, Edin and Kefalas (2005) documented the positive side of childbirth and how it made young mothers want to change their behaviors. They also found a link between motherhood and criminal desistance, and the participants had cognitive behavioral changes after finding out they were pregnant. They established a more positive outlook on life and wanted to make changes to provide a better life and future for their children.

Research and literature both reveal the negative outcomes and outlooks on teenage pregnancy and parenting, including poverty, lack of education, and inadequate social support (Furstenberg, Brooks-Gunn, and Morgan, 1987).

Lashley et al. (2009) studied the interaction and emotional bonds between urban African American mothers ages thirteen to twenty-one and their infants; they were found to be positive, with very little evidence that their transitions for the urban African American mothers were problematic, as found in previous studies. The African American mothers provided descriptions of their infants during their pregnancy and up to four months postpartum that resulted in positive associations with their infants. Their attitudes and behaviors have become increasingly positive over time. Lashley et al. concluded the mothers took pride in their children and viewed their relationships with their babies as important. Lashley et al. also found even though some of the pregnancies were not planned or expected, African American adolescent mothers experienced similar transitions to parenthood as did older women. Shanok and Miller (2007b) found that African American adolescent mothers felt having a baby, even though it was not planned, was positive for them because it made them have a different perspective on life. Shanok and Miller (2007b) found in their study on urban African American teen mothers that childbearing at a young age has had positive effects for those young women who were engaged in risky behaviors; having their baby gave them a better outlook on life. Previous phenomenological studies conducted on the urban teen mother population noted that the mothers stated that having their child had made them change their behaviors (Edin and Kefalas 2005; Klaw 2008; Wright and Davis 2008).

In their qualitative study, Brubaker and Wright (2006) demonstrated ways in which urban African American adolescent mothers were able to cope with their transition to motherhood—with the help and support of kinship and family members. For example, knowing they had support and resources eased the transitional stressors for them.

Stress and Young Motherhood

Childbirth is a natural occurrence that can result in positive or negative experiences and outcomes. A positive experience of childbirth is attributed to positive maternal attachment and engagement (Mercer 1986), while a negative childbirth experience results in the mother's inability to adapt to her maternal role, resulting in a strained relationship with her infant (Sauls 2004). While negative childbirth experiences vary from individual to individual,,Low et al. (2003)

found perceived traumatic experiences are related to short- and long-term implications from the mother's mental health status and parenting abilities. Clemmens (2002) found that depression affects adolescent mothers' ability to establish and maintain relationships with their infants. This, in turn, affects their ability to nurture and develop the security of their infants. Urban adolescent mothers live in areas that often lack resources and support, which tends to lead to high stress and depression (Borkowski, Whitman, and Farris 2007).

PTSD has been found to be linked with adolescent mother populations. Major depression, violence, substance abuse, maltreatment, and poor maternal attachment and parenting are all behaviors associated with PTSD in adolescent mothers (Abrams and Curran 2011; Ammerman et al. 2012; Sumner et al. 2012; Thompson and Massat 2005). Teens who report being in violent relationships from either childhood abuse or partner violence have been found to carry the memories and learned behaviors into motherhood. This often results in being depressed or exhibiting signs and symptoms of PTSD before, during, or after pregnancy (Anderson 2008). Adolescent mothers have expressed personal symptoms of isolation as well as abandonment (Clemmens 2002).

Adolescent mothers have been found to experience parenting problems and stress caused by unrealistic expectations of their child and their child's development (Milan et al. 2004). Current literature often characterizes adolescent motherhood and African American mothers' relationships with infants as problematic (Lashley et al. 2009). Behaviors and actions classifying adolescent motherhood have been found to be exaggerated or missing key elements that would provide viable interpretations of the mother's behaviors. Implications for early teen pregnancy are often magnified compared with adults to the limitations of financial resources, transitional experiences, lack of education obtainment, and deficient interpersonal parenting skills—leaving a negative impression that African American adolescent mothers are incapable of proper parenting (Benson 2004). Benson noted that prior research found pregnant teens reveal higher levels of family dysfunction and reported poorer communication skills;

however, the teens were able to overcome these dilemmas with support. Several studies found a link between lower level of family support and depression in teens (Davis, Rhodes, and Hamilton-Leaks 1997; Lanzi et al. 2009; Stevenson, Maton, and Tei 1999).

Parenting Stressors and Young Motherhood

Adolescent mothers handle the transition of becoming a mother in various ways. Research identifies varying results with the process. Noria et al. (2007) found the difficulties of navigating the paths from teen mother to adulthood can lead to problems with psychological adjustment, often resulting in poor parenting practices and a struggle to complete education goals, along with achieving economic self-sufficiency (p. 37). Noria et al. also found that the teen mother's inability to cope with stressful life events related to becoming a mother can lead to chronic depression and a rejection of their parental role. In a previous comparative study of first-time teen mothers and adult mothers, Whitman et al. (2001) found that teenage mothers struggle more than adult mothers with low esteem, anxiety, and depression. Supportive individuals such as mothers, caretakers, and others who provide emotional support show the mentee has increased levels of self-esteem, anxiety, and depression. That concept is in accordance with what Shanok and Miller (2007b) found in their study of adolescent mothers; the adolescent mothers found a constellation of support in their mothers and grandmothers.

Adolescent mothers are often prone to elevated levels of emotional distress because of their increased levels of parenting responsibilities (Milan et al. 2004). They have also been found to experience stress and display parenting problems because of their unrealistic expectations of their child and their child's development (Milan et al. 2004). As adolescent mothers attempt to adjust to their role of becoming a mother, they are sometimes plagued with depressive symptoms, high levels of stress, a sense of hopelessness, and, in some cases, PTSD, (Meadows-Oliver et al. 2007). Early transition into parenting provides little opportunity for the necessary preparation needed to properly parent a child. The consequences of early parenting led to increased economic burdens and reduced educational obtainment for adolescent mothers. Before pregnancy, urban young mothers often suffer from financial strains; early childbearing leads to additional strain and reduced resources and support (Booth et al. 2008; Chang and Fine 2007; Sangalang 2006).

Motherhood can be stressful for new mothers, particularly adolescent ones (Budd et al. 2006; Holub et al. 2007; Oxford et al. 2010). Mothers often report feeling overwhelmed and highly stressed. If left untreated, the stressors can result in traumatic experiences for their children. Holub et al. (2007) found that adolescents were at increased risk for maternal adjustment and postpartum depression when they experienced high levels of stress during and after pregnancy. Holub et al. defined adolescent maternal adjustment as feelings about infant care, parenting competency, and motherhood. The study concluded that there was a continuous need for early intervention programs to assist adolescent mothers with increased maternal adjustment and services to help them lessen emotional distress.

In addition, according to a 2009 report from the advocacy group Every Child Matters, in 2007 a reported 1,760 children died from maltreatment in the United States, an increase of 35 percent since 2001 (Barker 2009). The report also showed that cases involving abuse and neglect increased as much as 50 percent because of the poor data collection from local stage agencies. Further investigation of the rates revealed a parent was the perpetrator in 70 percent of fatalities. The mother's demographics were often that she was poor, lacking a high school diploma, was a young adult, and had first-hand experience of violence. Barker also noted that the single best predictor of child abuse and neglect was poverty due to associated risk factors, such as poor housing, low education, mental illness, teen parenthood, unemployment, and many other social ills that plague American society.

Research clearly shows that when adolescent mothers have emotional and financial support and basic resources, their levels of depression and anxiety are lower compared with adolescent mothers who do not have that support (Bartlett and Easterbrooks 2012; Boden, Fergusson, and Horwood 2008; Kennedy and Bennett 2006; Milan et al. 2004). Failure to meet the adolescent mother's emotional needs and lack of supervision, guidance, and support often promote stress, elevated levels of anxiety, and depressive symptomology (Eshbaugh et al. 2006; Holub et al. 2007; Meadows-Oliver, Swartz, and Krause 2007; Pinto-Foltz, Lodgson, and Derrick 2011).

These behaviors in turn often result in poor parenting practices and, in some cases, child abuse and neglect (Bert et al. 2009; Lee 2009; Lounds et al. 2006).

Emotional Factors Associated with Becoming a Mother

Adolescent mothers must endure the interruption of their teen life and take on the responsibilities and duties associated with adult parenthood. The emotional factors associated with the development of the dual identity have been analyzed. Adolescent mothers have found that their new roles as parents often bring a great deal of stress and social-emotional maladjustment (Logsdon et al. 2008). The psychosocial adjustments endured by teen mothers once they give birth include various clinical diagnoses, including depression (Knoche et al. 2007). Early childbearing in adolescents also contributes to the onset of additional interpersonal challenges of parenting, including physical exhaustion, social isolation from family and friends, and lack of support (Birkeland et al. 2005).

Depression and Adolescent Motherhood

Pregnant and parenting adolescent mothers experience high levels of stress that often overwhelm and deplete their emotional drives, leaving them with no energy for role identity development, self-conception stabilization, or the opportunity to enhance or work on any other developmental task (Erikson 1968; Eshbaugh et al. 2006). Unresolved developmental tasks, stress of identity development, and attempts to fit in to new maternal roles are all factors that, along with others, tend to lead to depression in adolescent mothers. In addition, these mothers often feel overwhelmed by coping with the social, physical, and psychological challenges endured during their adolescent development. Tending to the new duties, responsibilities, and needs of their child has also been found to be a stress-inducing event, which precipitated depressive symptoms (Edwards et al. 2012; Eshbaugh et al. 2006; Stevenson et al. 1999).

Early childbearing has been found to cause extreme emotional setbacks for adolescent mothers. Previous research has found the new role often brings on traumatic social-emotional distress and maladjustment (Borkowski et al. 2002; Caldwell, Antonucci, and Jackson 1998; Eshbaugh 2006; Knoche et al. 2007; Shanok and Miller 2005). The emotional distress of birth and delivery was found to be a traumatic experience for young mothers. Coupled with lack of preparedness (financially, emotionally, or socially) in providing for their babies, emotions and feelings translated to depression (Borkowski et al. 2002; Sadler and Cowlin 2003; Stiles 2010). Birkeland et al. (2005) concurred and found the role of new parent for adolescent mothers includes the challenges and feelings of physical exhaustion, isolation from family and friends, lack of support, and interpersonal challenges that cause depressive symptoms. Early childbearing for teen mothers has been found to result in tremendous emotional states—behaviors that often translate into depression and extreme emotional distress.

The transition from being a teenager to upholding the new rules of being a *parent* is a difficult process because of teen mothers' cognitive inability to think like a responsible adult/parent, their lack of maturity, and their ongoing development as a teen and young adult, which exemplifies self-centered behaviors (Easterbrooks, Chaudhuri, and Gestsdottir 2005; Sadler and Cowlin 2003; Sommer et al. 1993). The pressures of undertaking a new role and identity when they are in the process of still developing their own self-identities are challenging (Brubaker and Wright 2006). Lewin et al. (2011) found that young African American mothers have additional components linked to increased depression. These include enduring multiple sources of context stressors, such as being victims of violence or ethnic discrimination. Similarly, Goodman and Aber (2010) found that adolescent mothers need social support and individual interventions to assist them with ameliorating their depressive symptoms. Depression resulted from the overwhelming duties and responsibilities of parenting, and it was often the result of having to endure traumatic experiences. Representational aggression in preschool children of low-income, urban, African American adolescent mothers were significantly correlated with the child's gender (male), child's birth weight, mother's educational level, mother's employment, maternal depression, mother's historical residency with own mothers, and feelings of social support. The findings suggested that predictors of poverty—such as lack of maternal educational attainment and increased levels of maternal depression during the first year of giving birth—were key factors in the pathways of existence of the representational aggression found in children with adolescent mothers (Goodman and Aber 2010).

Shanok and Miller (2007b) noted several problematic behaviors with teen mothers and their infants. Postpartum depression was found to be associated with negative effects in interacting with infants and less positive engagement with their infants. The negative engagements often led to increases in infant insecure attachment. Ispa et al. (2007) studied 173 low-income primiparous (pregnant for the first time) young African American mothers and their levels of warmth, parenting stress, and toddler attachment security. The study was conducted on women who were either pregnant or had given birth within one year of the study; their pregnancy acceptance and parenting stress were measured. The results revealed that one aspect of maternal parenting stress—the distress from feeling the burden of parenting—was a negative predictor for security for the toddler's attachment (Ispa et al. 2007).

Motherhood is overwhelming for adult women as well as for adolescent women (Mercer 2004).

Hormonal changes and ecological factors often have an effect on the mother's emotional and mental states. Motherhood is also overwhelming for adolescent mothers who are coping with the physical, social, and psychological aspects of adolescent development along with attempting to parent a child (Edwards et al. 2012; Eshbaugh 2006; Stevenson et al.1999; Stiles 2010). In their attempt to adjust to their new roles, adolescent mothers have been found to experience higher levels of depression than adult women (Gaines et al. 2009; Whitman et al. 2001). The literature identifies key factors attributable to depression in adolescent motherhood (Barnett et al. 2008; Birkeland et al. 2005; Lanzi et al. 2009; Lesser, Koniak–Griffin, and Anderson 1999; Long 2009). First-time adolescent mothers often lack the necessary social support and experience higher levels of stress (Hofferth and Goldscheider 2010). This situation precipitates increased levels of depression, which is more likely to lead to poor parenting practices resulting in abuse and neglect (Lanzi et al. 2009).

Lanzi et al. found that compared with adult mothers, first–time adolescent mothers displayed higher levels of depression within the first six months after giving birth, in addition to being constantly depressed at a level two times higher than adult mothers. The study also revealed that after the babies were born, the adolescent mother's depression increased, and they scored less favorably in general on verbal cues and maternal warmth. Their children scored less favorably in seeking warmth from their mothers. Maternal depression has been associated with increased interpersonal conflicts, risk of child abuse and neglect, decreased psychosocial functioning, and delayed child development (Barnet et al. 2008; Easterbrooks et al. 2010; Lanzi et al. 2009).

Support

Young mothers often lack resources and stable support systems. This can leave them living in poor conditions, lacking financial stability, and failing to achieve educational goals (Letourneau et al. 2004).

The lack of financial, emotional, and supportive resources often hinders young mothers from overcoming hurdles encountered during early childbearing (Shanok and Miller 2005). The concept of support derives from various methods and ideologies.

Letourneau et al. defined *social support* as interactions with family members, peers, and health professionals with whom the mother shares and communicates aid and understanding, esteem, and information. Social supports include professionals, peers, family members, and partners; modes include one-to-one interactions and groups of various frequencies and durations. When young mothers have social supports in their lives—especially during their transition to motherhood—they are more likely to be successful (Letourneau et al. 2004; Wright and Davis 2008).

Self-Identity and Motherhood

The seminal research conducted by Hurlburt and McDonald (1997) was one of the first studies to examine the multidimensional levels of adolescent parenthood. The study examined the transition of adolescence to motherhood, the disturbance of adolescence and role identity, and the effects the transition and role identity have on parenting attitudes. A similar study by Zimmer et al. (2001) focused on the psychosocial outcome of adolescents born to teen mothers and suggested further implications of research focus on the varying developmental phases of adolescent mothers rather than concentrating on their ages.

In the case of adolescent mothers, multiple and competing identities exist because the identity is influenced by others' perceptions (Hallman 2007).

The establishment of an identity is the epitome of adolescent development, along with the endurance of self-esteem and perceptions of peers, adults, and others. Adolescent mothers often have difficulty maintaining a psychological balance of determining their own identity, understanding and establishing a maternal identity, and attempting to counterbalance the negative perceptions of what other adults and their peers have of them since becoming pregnant or bearing a child (Noria et al. 2007). This process often leads to escalated numbers of adolescent mothers being depressed, frustrated, and feeling a sense of hopelessness. Adolescent mothers are often cast as feeling trapped or stuck because they are unsure of who they are or what they are supposed to do as mothers (Clemmens 2002; Knoche et al. 2007; Shanok and Miller 2007b).

McCrary and Weed (2005) discovered that adolescent mothers often struggle with identity formation compared with adult mothers in their early twenties. Their research yielded the following outcomes: 55 percent of the adolescent mothers were still attempting to establish beliefs and values or would accept beliefs without questioning them; 25 percent of the adult mothers were able to indicate commitment to values; and 65 percent of both adolescent and adult mothers' beliefs had periods when they had doubt and questions regarding their beliefs. A key element of the predicted identity development for both adolescent and adult mothers was the level of social support they received at the time of their pregnancy. Adolescent mothers often lacked adequate preparation for their parenting, which inevitably affected both mother and child (Whitman et al. 2001).

Dueling Identities

Adolescent mothers often find themselves in positions where they have to negotiate their teenage identity along with having to understand and identify as a mother and thinking and reasoning as a responsible adult (Aiello and Lancaster 2007; Hallman 2007; Lesser et al. 2003; Sadler and Cowlin 2003). During these periods, they are often forced to set aside egocentric teen urges of being a rebellious, self-absorbed, risk-taking youth and instead be willing to think about their child and their future (Kennedy 2006; Taylor 2010). Early childbearing interrupts the adolescent stage, which leaves adolescent mothers in a state of crisis because of their underdeveloped identity and forced state of intimacy and autonomy—both requirements of effective adult and parenthood (Erikson 1968). While struggling with the lack of parental preparation and simultaneously dealing with adolescent task development, pregnant adolescents are found to have increasingly higher levels of depression, frustration, and aggression compared with pregnant adults (Noria et al. 2007).

Adolescence is a developmental timeframe for self-exploration, self-indulgence, identity inquiry, and social experimentation. However, early motherhood and adolescent development often conflict because of the required duties and responsibilities and the lack of time for independence and individuation (Meadows-Oliver et al. 2007; Salder and Cowlin 2003). The dueling identities of adolescent motherhood do not allow room for compromise or negotiation because of the responsibilities employed by their roles. Being a mother requires specific duties, responsibilities, and continuity, which leave little room for the self-indulgence roles of being a teenager (Meadows-Oliver et al. 2007; Stiles 2010).

Furthermore, simultaneously attempting to cope with new parental roles and trying to handle their own teenage developmental task has been found to be a challenge for urban adolescent mothers. In turn, it creates high levels of anxiety and stress (Shanok and Miller 2007b). In addition, the adjustment from indulging to executing parenting duties and responsibilities has been found to lead to younger mothers experiencing higher levels of parental stress. This accounts for higher levels of poor parenting practices and poor developmental milestones for their children (Bornstein and Putnick 2007; Long 2009).

Birkeland et al. (2005) found because of the adjustment of distinctive personal and social changes for adolescent mothers, their first year postpartum leads to lower levels of self-esteem and increased levels of depression. Easterbrooks et al. (2005) endorsed the idea that adolescent mothers express desires and vocalize their needs when engaged in early childbearing that spans both emotionally and psychologically over periods of adolescence and adulthood.

Hallman (2007) studied the effects of reassigning the identity of pregnant and parenting teen mothers in a school setting. The findings revealed three themes that conceptualized the identity development of the pregnant and parenting students:

(a) students can learn to position themselves as mothers and students, (b) the school should be a place to learn as well as a community where adolescent mothers can receive additional emotional support and information regarding resources, and (c) young mothers provided with the assistance of daycare at the school gave hope for a better future for both mother and child. Hallman examined the correlations between literacy and identity development. She focused on the connection between literacy and identity to assist educators in recognizing how pregnant and parenting students reveal different levels of their identities according to the context in which they find themselves. Hallman affirmed the multifaceted roles adolescent mothers portray—that of mother, student, and adolescent. This enabled educators to assist and educate pregnant and parenting students, which enabled the mother's academic success in school (Hallman 2007).

Resilience

The research has overstated numerous negative outcomes for early childbearing and the strains it often has on young mothers (Jacobs and Mollborn 2012; SmithBattle 2013). Masten, Best, and Garmezy (1990) referred to *resilience* as successful adaptation despite exposure to risk or stressors. Borkowski, Whitman, and Farris (2007) defined the concept in three ways: (a) resilience refers to the process or pattern of adaptation rather than a characteristic of a person per se, (b) resilience is based on the inferences regarding the ability to adapt in the face of adversity, and (c) the person engaging in resilient behavior must be judged as functioning adequately.

Overall, adolescent mothers have been faced with risks and stressors as a result of early childbearing, but they have also demonstrated levels of perseverance (despite the lack of support and resources) and the ability to complete their educations and maintain employment (Oxford et al. 2007; SmithBattle and Lenard 2007,

2012). The short-term effects of early childbearing are one avenue; however, there are stories of resiliency and overcoming the hurdles of early childbearing (Brubaker and Wright 2006; Wright and Davis 2008). The Furstenberg et al. 1987 longitudinal study has put to rest the theory that early childbearing has a destructive and devastating end; the depictions of young mothers are often exaggerated (Oxford et al. 2010; SmithBattle 2013). Furstenberg et al. revealed many of the young mothers go on to have additional children, complete school and even further their educations, get married, and lead successful lives.

Some key factors assist the young mothers in being resilient and not succumbing to the difficulties they face. Financial, social, and emotional supports are all key elements that help young mothers overcome their hurdles (Eshbaugh-Soha and Peake 2011; SmithBattle 2013; SmithBattle and Leonard 2012). Research documenting the negative outcomes and consequences of early childbearing among adolescents dominates the literature on adolescent childbearing (Coley and Chase-Lansdale 1998; Driscoll et al. 2005; Furstenberg et al. 1987; Henretta 2007; Taylor 2010; Whitman et al. 2001); however, adolescent mothers still manage to prevail and triumph over the hurdles (Jacobs and Mollborn 2012; Lesser et al. 2003; Milan et al. 2004; Shanok and Miller 2007a; Wright and Davis 2008). Milan et al. (2004) found that interventions that focus on interpersonal factors assist pregnant and parenting adolescents with their transitions. Interpersonal factors include relational figures who play a significant role in the emotional development of adolescent mothers. Easterbrooks et al. (2010) took a further look into what makes young mothers resiliency in adolescent mother that lack of education, poverty, increased involvement in crime, poor parenting practices, potential risk, harm brought to their children, and so on. They used an approach focused primarily on the adolescent mother to examine parenting skills among mothers younger than twenty-one. They defined *resilient functioning* as a parent who lacks the perpetration of child maltreatment in the context of risk. Risk factors were evaluated at various levels and included ecological factors and negative family childhood histories. Ecological factors included financial stressors of the mother and neighborhood poverty (Anthony 2008; Kennedy 2006; Kreager et al. 2010; Roche, Ensminger, and Cherlin 2007; SmithBattle and Leonard 2012). The results revealed that groups of mothers demonstrated resiliency despite the ecological risk factors and family trajectories. The data also showed that resilient mothers had higher levels of depression, which suggested there was a cost for engaging in resilient parenting functioning. The resilient mothers were not perpetrators of child maltreatment, which is often a factor in highly stressed mothers (Borkowski, Whitman, and Farris 2007; Lee 2009).

Summary

Becoming a mother is a monumental phase in a woman's life that includes developmental changes and varying psychological tasks (Mercer 2004). Naturally, most women describe their infants in positive terms during pregnancy and in their newborn period, during which their babies bring joy and excitement to the mother (Mercer 2004). Teen parenting often brings an enormous number of stressors and logistical barriers (Shanok and Miller 2005). The experience of becoming a mother is a developmentally normal and natural occurrence in a woman's life, but it can also be an extremely stressful event (Copeland and Harbaugh 2010). The dynamics of adolescent motherhood have an adverse effect on mother and child (Larson 2004). During the adolescent stage of development, adolescents experience an increase in depression, anxiety, and hostility—all of which overlap during the stage (Milan et al. 2004). Studies have examined the symptoms of depression (Milan et al. 2004) and concluded that negative outcomes of teen parenting include parenting difficulty, negative child outcomes, and poorer newborn health. Investigating the emotional distresses experienced by teen mothers in a broader scope offers a better constellation and true depiction of functioning adolescent mothers.

Adolescent mothers experience numerous interpersonal dilemmas during their pregnancy and postpartum period (Florsheim et al. 2003). The transition to motherhood requires interpersonal factors such as resolving relationship conflicts, getting early caregiving experiences, and identifying social supports (SmithBattle and Leonard 2012). The developmental process adolescent mothers endure as they transition from teens to mothers often occurs within a relational context, and these factors play a significant role in the success of the mother's adjustment (Florsheim et al. 2003). The common themes that resonate in the literature relating to the adolescent mother's stress are depression, anxiety, and parenting stressors.

Chapter 3 will provide details of the methodological components used for the qualitative research study. It will describe the qualitative research methods and design used to capture the experiences of urban adolescent mothers as they transition from being teens to being mothers. The chapter will provide details of the sampling processes used for data collection along with the theoretical concepts that were selected to examine the outcomes. The research study's limitations, credibility, expected findings, and ethical concerns will all be addressed at the end of the chapter.

Chapter 3

METHODS AND PROCEDURES

This chapter provides the methodology, discussions of the research methods and procedures, and the selection process for the sample populations. It also describes the methods for data collection and analysis used for the current study. Finally, the chapter discusses ethical considerations and limitations, and it ends with a brief summary.

Adolescent mothers endure a battle of dualism; they have to balance an evolving self-identity while also developing a maternal-role identity. This battle leaves them in a state of crisis and confusion when attempting to balance both identities simultaneously (Noria et al. 2009). The current study used a phenomenological research design to explore the experiences of urban adolescent mothers as they transitioned into motherhood and developed maternal identity. In an attempt to identify experiences of individuals regarding a particular phenomenon, Moustakas (1994) asserted that to obtain a comprehensive description, one has to return to the experience. Therefore, as people talk about and describe their experiences, an understanding of the phenomenon being studied unfolds. Creswell (2007) also noted that a phenomenological study describes the meaning for several individuals of their experiences as a concept or a phenomenon. The basic purpose of phenomenology is to reduce individual experiences with a phenomenon to a description of the universal essence (Creswell 2007). In this study, the thoughts, perceptions, feelings, and experiences of urban adolescent mothers were captured through their eyes as they transitioned from being teens to becoming mothers and developing maternal-role identity. Their descriptions were captured with the use of semistructured interviews. The participants had an opportunity to provide the researcher with an in-depth look at personal, social, and emotional factors involved with their evolution of becoming mothers while they were adolescents.

The experiences of the transition from adolescent to mother and the phenomenon of the transitional process in developing maternal-role identity were elicited from urban, adolescent mothers ages eighteen to twenty-two who had given birth within thirty-six months at the time of the study. The data was collected through the use of face-to-face, in-depth interviews in a private and trusting environment where the participants were able to divulge their personal experiences. The interviews took place in classrooms at a daycare and vocational center, where permission was granted by program directors. The interview questions were used to guide the interview process, which allotted time for the researcher to generate adequate data for a clearer understanding of the phenomenon. To determine validity of the interview questions, a field test was conducted with experts familiar with the adolescent mother population. The researcher used a licensed professional counselor who was the clinical program coordinator of an urban teen mother program and was familiar with the population characteristics. Also assisting were three doctoral-level researchers who specialize in this area of research; they examined the questions and checked them for validity. All of the panelists suggested using less academic and more basic wording for the interview questions, so the participants would be able to understand the questions. The results of this field test were revised interview questions; all panelists scored the new questions with high ratings.

In an attempt to gain a better understanding of the phenomenon, the following interview questions were asked:

1. How did your life change after your baby was born? (examples)

2. What are some of the challenges you faced after having your baby?

3. Tell me (describe) about your transition from being a teen to being a teen mother.

4. Describe the feelings or emotions you experienced in your new role of being a mother.

5. What would you say was the most challenging part about being a teen mother, and how did you overcome the challenges?

6. Tell me about the positive experiences you have experienced since becoming a mother.

7. Describe a moment that made you feel proud about yourself as a mother.

Method

Research Method and Design

The study employed a qualitative research method and used the phenomenological approach adapted from Giorgi (1985, 2009), Moustakas (1994), and Stones (1979). The objective was to capture the essence of the phenomenon that urban adolescent mothers endure as they transform from being a teen to becoming a mother. A qualitative methodology design was best suited for this study because an attempt was made to understand the experiences of the transitioning process, perceptions, and perspectives of adolescent mothers as they develop and emerge into becoming mothers. The phenomenological approach attempts to answer questions by capturing the essences of a particular life experience, concept, or phenomenon (Moustakas 1994); this is achieved by the participants' first revealing their individual transitional experiences as urban adolescent mothers and then developing a description of the universal essence (Moustakas 1994). Stones (1979) also asserted that the phenomenological researcher's goal is to describe the phenomenon as it appears rather than explaining it through preexisting frameworks.

In this case, the description would consist of the identified elements and factors experienced during the transition to motherhood.

Phenomenological Research

The phenomenological approach seeks to uncover certain behaviors of the experiences as they take place. The researcher is responsible for interpreting the given descriptions of the situation in which the behavior and the experiences occur.

Moustakas (1994) asserted that the empirical phenomenological approach involves a return to an experience to obtain comprehensive descriptions. These descriptions provide the basis for a reflective structural analysis that portrays the essences of the experience.

Phenomenology also explores the perspectives of those who went through the experience by adapting a strictly descriptive approach (Giorgi 1985). Creswell (2007) described a *phenomenology study* as the meaning for specific groups of individuals to share their experiences of a concept or a phenomenon, therefore reducing individual experiences to a universal essence.

This study examined the ongoing problems of adjustment often experienced by urban adolescent mothers as they transition from adolescent to motherhood. The ecological factors of living in urban areas and neighborhoods as external and internal stressors have been found to have a direct impact on the social and psychological well-being of African American adolescents (Taylor 2011). Early childbearing has been found to have negative effects on urban adolescent mothers. However, the issues of resilience and overcoming challenges are often clouded by negative physical outcomes, such as abuse and neglect of their children, poverty, unemployment, and lack of education (Geronimus 2003; Hurd and Zimmerman 2010). By engaging in face-to-face interviews and developing a better understanding of the psychological experiences shared by urban adolescent mothers, it was anticipated that the knowledge of their experiences would allow room for formal systematic changes in services—or the ability to establish better resources than those currently offered to teen mothers.

Establishing an understanding of the duality of identity often experienced by urban adolescent mothers could assist social service localities in providing more extensive programming to assist teen mothers with the psychological effects of early childbearing (Kaye 2008; Oxford et al. 2010). It is also considered imperative for researchers to gather an understanding of the adolescent mother's transitioning into a mother—while being forced to shed an undeveloped adolescent persona and being forced to take on an additional persona of a "responsible" adult in which one has limited cognitive and perceptual abilities (Luong 2008.) The use of the phenomenological research method assisted this researcher in gathering and developing an understanding in the women's true voices—the experiences and the deliberations of the urban adolescent mothers as they transition into motherhood.

Rationale for Qualitative Research Design

Within the framework of a qualitative approach, the phenomenological research design was best suited for this study. The study sought to examine the perceptions, thoughts, feelings, and experiences of urban adolescent mothers and their transition to motherhood. In-depth interviews in a trusting environment were used to extract details from urban adolescent mothers of their experiences postpartum and how they came to terms with being mothers. Qualitative methodology emphasizes the importance of unearthing an experience and account that took place. The intentions are commonly focused on extracting and interpreting the meaning of the actual experience (Denzin and Lincoln 2003).

Obtaining a basic understanding is the primary goal of qualitative research, and the researcher is the instrument for data collection and analysis (Bloomberg and Volpe 2008). An underlying assumption of qualitative research is that the data collected is neither stable nor uniform; therefore, many truths are often left up to interpretation.

Qualitative data are analyzed inductively, which requires flexibility in the research design. In this case, the use of a phenomenological approach was best suited. Moustakas (1994) recommended the use of a systematic data analysis procedure that incorporates significant statements, meanings, and themes—as well as an extensive description—to capture the true essence of the phenomenon when using phenomenological study.

In-depth, face-to-face interviews were used to gather and collect data. The interviews took place in a safe and trusting environment that allowed participants to disclose their experiences of transitioning into motherhood. Interviews are a form of data collection for qualitative research (Creswell 2007; Merriam 2009). Interviewing is necessary when behavior cannot be observed (Patton 2002). This researcher used phenomenological methods to analyze and reveal biases and attempted to create intimate and self-revealing conversation. With the guidance of phenomenological methods of interviewing, the researcher attempted to uncover the essence of the adolescent mother's experience. During the interview process, the interviewer focused on the profound meanings that events have for individuals, assuming they are guided by actions and interactions (Marshall and Rossman 2006). The face-to-face interviews with the urban adolescent mothers helped the researcher uncover the essential essences and meanings of the adolescent mother's conquest of maternal-role identity and development.

The researcher collected and analyzed the data with the use of an audio recorder. She interviewed the participants individually face-to-face for forty-five to sixty minutes. The researcher transcribed the interviews and prepared transcripts for the participants to review for accuracy, thus using a triangulation process to review the collected data. The researcher also collaborated with an external auditor who was familiar with qualitative data research when used during data analysis (identifying meaning units from the transcripts and making the conversion into themes). The audit trail was considered to be a systematically maintained documentation system. After successful completion of the triangulation process, data files were created.

They consisted of organization of the data to include filing, creating a computer database, and breaking large units into smaller ones (Creswell 1998).

As a program director, co-owner of a teen mother residential program, and a state board licensed professional counselor, this researcher has witnessed numerous accounts of trials and tribulations of adolescent mothers as they struggle to adapt to their new roles and responsibilities of motherhood. The researcher has witnessed countless efforts of intentional selfish acts and motives bestowed on the adolescents' children. She has engaged in numerous hours of conversations with adolescent mothers as they struggled with feelings of betrayal, burden, and grief handling the responsibilities of motherhood, while witnessing their teenage years wither away in front of them. The purpose of the study was to capture the true essence, feelings, and experiences of individual adolescent mothers as they embarked on their road to motherhood. It was the aim of the researcher to capture and interpret the phenomenon with an unbiased, objective viewpoint and to suspend any preconceived notions of personal experiences that might influence her (Leedy and Ormrod 2010). To avoid the invasion of personal experiences, the researcher used bracketing or *epoché*, which is when the investigator sets aside personal experiences and notions to take a fresh perspective toward the phenomenon under examination (Moustakas 1994; Creswell 2007).

An ontological assumption was used for this proposed research study. The ontological assumption asks the question "What is the nature of reality?" and refers to the nature of social reality. *Ontology* is the study of "claims and assumptions that are made about the nature of social reality, claims about what exists, what it looks like, what units make it up and how these units interact with each other" (Grix 2004, 34). For the purpose of this study, the researcher attempted to capture the reality of the transition as experienced by adolescent mothers. The goal was to capture and interpret the true factors and elements of the adolescents' transition to motherhood—derived from their direct perspectives.

The concepts from the interpretivist perspective guided the current study. With the use of the interpretivism paradigm, Mack (2010) asserted that the researcher can never objectively observe from the outside; rather, the researcher must observe from inside through the direct experience of the subjects.

The role of the researcher in the interpretivist paradigm is to view the social reality through the eyes of different participants while understanding, explaining, and demystifying the social reality. The researcher using the interpretivist paradigm sets out to seek to understand rather than to explain (Cohen, Manion, and Morrison 2007). The main ontological assumptions of the interpretivist paradigm suggest:

(a) reality is indirectly constructed based on individual interpretation and is subjective, (b) people interpret and make their own meaning of events, (c) events are distinctive and cannot be generalized, (d) there are multiple perspectives on one incident, and (e) causation in social sciences is determined by interpreted meaning and symbols (Mack 2010).

The goal of this study was to capture, identify, and understand the perceptions, thoughts, feelings, and experiences of urban adolescent mothers' transitional process of becoming a mother and developing their maternal-role identity; therefore, a phenomenological approach was the suitable research method to use to gather and collect data. The current research study was guided by theoretical frameworks of psychosocial development stages by Erikson with elements of the Mercer's (2004) BAM theory and the conceptual model by Kaiser and Hays (2004). Erikson's psychosocial development theory reveals eight stages that individual's transition throughout their life spans. The fourth stage is the adolescent stage, which is defined as the identity versus role confusion stage. It involves individuals establishing a clear understanding of their identity and the roles they are to portray. If they do not successfully complete the stage, they are left in crisis, which results in role confusion (Erikson 1968). Kaiser and Hays (2004) developed the conceptual model, which emphasized the prenatal and postpartum effects of motherhood on adolescent mothers. The model emphasized the dual developmentalism often experienced by adolescent mothers. The dual developmentalism represents the developmental task of adolescence and the simultaneous developmental task of becoming a mother.

Kaiser and Hays (2004) identified four psychosocial factors that affect the transition to motherhood in teens during the prenatal and postpartum period: (a) gaining acceptance of their pregnancy, (b) planning for the future, (c) viewing self as mother, and (d) growing up and seeing things as an adult. Those four concepts were used as a guide to identify the effect of the transition on the adolescent mothers as they developed and gained acceptance of their maternal roles.

The study also used the elements of Mercer's (2004) BAM theory to assist with determining the transitional factors associated with the adolescent mother's acceptance of her maternal-role identity. Mercer found that the development of maternal identity is influenced by the mother's self-concept and personality traits, such as the ability to be flexible and to show empathy for her child. Mercer (2004) found teen mothers struggle to achieve a maternal role because of variables such as marital status, psychosocial immaturity, ignorance of parenting skills, and faulty expectations of their infants' developmental maturity. Mercer also found that circumstantial factors—such as poverty, low educational attainment, and lack of social support—are key factors that directly affect the experience of becoming a mother. The demographic factors associated with urban living play a key role in understanding how ecological factors affect the transitional process of maternal role development.

Selection of Participants

The research was conducted in an eastern urban city. The location currently has one of the highest rates of teen pregnancy—as well as nonmarital births—within the Commonwealth of Virginia (Health Department 2012). The 2009 rate of resident teen pregnancy was 70.1 per thousand compared with the average state rate of 24.3 per thousand (VDH, Center for Health Statistics, n.d.). Nearly half of all nonmarital first births occur to teens. In fact, teenagers who have a nonmarital birth are significantly less likely to be married by the age of thirty-five.

The participation selection process was based on established criteria required for this study. The study's criteria selection for participation included adolescent mothers between the ages of eighteen and twenty-two who had given birth to a child within the last thirty-six months. The participants were required to reside in the city where the study took place and had to have the cognitive and mental capacity to answer oral questions for forty-five to sixty minutes. Exclusionary criteria consisted of the following: not signing, not completing, or not submitting a consent form; women under eighteen or older than twenty-three; women who were pregnant; women who were unable to participate in the oral interview for the allotted time of forty-five to sixty minutes; and women who were unwilling to share their transitional thoughts, perceptions, emotions, or experiences of their maternal-role identity development.

The researcher has established professional relationships with numerous organizations that provide services to young unwed mothers.

The study's target population was selected from a general population of young single mothers who participate in a local, urban city outreach program. The program provides vocational guidance, educational training, and general assistance to a high population of young, single mothers and has a local daycare center that many single mothers use.

Permission to solicit the participants was requested and granted by the owner of the two day-care programs. The owners of the programs gave permission to the researcher to solicit teen mothers over the age of eighteen as participants for the study. An additional meeting was held with the program directors to provide information, explain the research process, and establish the date for participant selection. The researcher provided the program directors with a letter inviting the potential participants to an informational session, which provided an overview of the study.

The flyer included contact information for the researcher, an explanation of the research study and requirements, information on confidentiality, and informed consent requirements. The interviews took place on-site in private classrooms.

The concept of purposeful sampling is often used for qualitative research (Creswell 2007; Leedy and Ormrod 2010); however, for phenomenological studies, Creswell suggested using a more narrow range of sampling strategies with as many as ten individuals. Purposive sampling was used because of the specified population and the fact that the quality of the participants—rather that quantity—has a bearing on the outcome. The object of the study was to become "saturated" with the information pertaining to the transitional experiences of adolescents becoming mothers.

The researcher used a sample population of ten to fifteen participants until saturation was reached. Wargo (2012) described the use of interviews as tools to gather data. When the number of participants is low, usually around ten participants are ideal—or until saturation is achieved. Saturation is a concept or realization that researchers experience during the interview process with multiple participants; at a certain point, no new meaning units are emerging. At this point, data collection can be terminated (Corbin and Strauss 2008).

Data Collection

For phenomenological study, the data collection process consists of gathering information through in-depth interviews with at least ten individuals (Creswell 2007). The face-to-face interviews were used to collect data from adolescent mothers about their transition from being teenagers to becoming mothers. Creswell (1994) found that an interview also gives the researcher the opportunity to clarify responses and probe for additional information.

Although interviews are an ideal form of data collection for phenomenological studies, they can pose limitations as well (Wargo 2012). One limitation was that participants were limited to urban adolescent mothers, which limits the ability to apply the results to regional or statewide issues concerning adolescent mothers.

The participants received contact information with phone numbers, addresses, and e-mail addresses of two state-licensed mental health providers for any additional services that might be needed. The researcher used a nonconfrontational approach with the participants to assist with the difficult questions and to establish and maintain a rapport with them (Leedy and Ormrod 2010). The participants had to recall their personal experiences. It was assumed that they were willing to remember and share all of the emotional and behavioral factors experienced during their transition—,which brings up the concern of trustworthiness.

Trustworthiness is a major threat and limitation in a study like this. The participants may say what they believe the researcher wants them to say or what they think is the "correct response" without disclosing the factual situation (Leedy and Ormond 2010).

The researcher ensured the participants of confidentiality by assigning code names to each one; only the researcher maintained the list with the original names and assignments. The demographic information and materials for the interview were kept in a locked file cabinet in the researcher's private office. Also, the transcribed interviews were kept on a double-password-secured computer also located in the researcher's office. The researcher also explained the significance of the study, which alleviated participants' concern that any nonfactual information might be disclosed.

Individual in-depth semistructured interviews were given to young mothers ages eighteen to twenty-two in a private office. The interviews consisted of open-ended questions that enabled the participant the opportunity to fully answer the questions. In-depth interviews were audiotaped and captured the transitional experience of becoming a mother while being an adolescent.

All interviews were aligned with the identified measured concepts: emotional factors, associated characteristics or behaviors, and coping mechanisms used during the transitional phase of becoming a mother. The participants had free will to respond to the questions and reveal their personal accounts. Each participant gave her personal story of her transition from an adolescent to becoming a mother. The data analysis process consisted of identifying common themes mentioned in the interviews and the descriptions of their experiences. Each interview was also transcribed using a method suggested by Wargo (2012):

1. The transcripts were typed with consecutive line numbers for the entire manuscript. Both the researcher and participants' dialogues were included. The page numbers were included along with the right margins, which were 2–2 1/2 inches wide.
2. A code name or number was assigned at the top of all transcriptions.
3. Recordings were listened to as the researcher read the transcripts. The interviews were typed as they were heard.

The process for narrowing down the themes consisted of the following (Creswell 2007): identifying the statements related to the topic, grouping the statements into "meaningful units," seeking divergent perspectives, and constructing a composite. The result is a general description of the transitional phenomenon as it is revealed and related through the eyes and voice.

The researcher interviewed the participants in designated private classrooms assigned by each of the organizations. The researcher read the consent form to each candidate and obtained her consent to participate in the study by signature. After the consent was obtained, the researcher discussed the research project and the process, risks, benefits, and confidentiality. The researcher asked general questions about the participant to make her feel relaxed. Before beginning, the researcher also gave the participant the opportunity to opt out of the study. The researcher gave the participant an opportunity to ask additional questions before beginning the interview, and began with general conversation to put her at ease.

The participant was informed again of the research process, which consisted of the interviews, an additional meeting to share the transcript of the data for verification, and permission to use the interpretations as presented. Any information identified as incorrect would not be used.

The interviews took forty-five minutes to one hour in a semistructured interview process with the use of a prepared interview guide to assist in asking questions. Rubin and Babbie (2001) suggested the use of an interview guide consisting of a list of the research questions asked during the interview. The use of the guide provided more structure than a completely unstructured, informal conversational interview while maintaining a relatively high degree of flexibility.

Once recruited, the participants notified the researcher via telephone if they were interested in participating. The researcher developed a screening questionnaire to determine whether the participant met the requirements to participate in the study. The screening script consisted of the following questions:

1. What is your date of birth?
2. What is the age of your child?
3. Are you the primary caretaker of your child?
4. Are you willing to sit for a face-to-face interview for about one hour, with possible additional time of up to one hour after the interview?
5. Are you willing to discuss your personal experiences of what it was like becoming a mother?
6. Do you have any concerns or worries that discussing your experiences may cause you to have an emotional reaction?

After verifying that participants met the screening criteria, the researcher scheduled the interview. Before the interview began, the researcher read the consent form aloud to the potential participant and discussed its contents. The participant was asked to sign the consent form, and the research process began. Demographic information was gathered with the use of a brief questionnaire asking for the following information: age at the birth of the first child, highest level of education completed and date of completion, current income/subsidies, and area in the city in which they live.

The researcher asked whether the participant had any other questions about the process or the research before beginning the actual session. This question was posed to ease any apprehension or tension between the researcher and participant. The researcher used an interview guide to ask about the feelings and emotions surrounding the pregnancy, giving birth, changes of life experienced, postpartum care and support, and feelings about themselves and their roles—and their feelings about their new roles as mothers. The research guide contained all of the prescribed interview questions and served as a reference guide during the interview.

Three doctoral-level researchers and a licensed professional counselor reviewed the interview questions, and some original questions were changed to align with the research topics. Wording was changed to ensure clear comprehension by participants, based on educational levels. Finally, it was suggested that the questions mimic the topic and themes of the research questions, purpose of the study, and problem statement. This was done to ensure the true phenomenon was being captured from the participants' responses.

Therefore, in an attempt to gain a better understanding of the phenomenon, the following interview questions were asked:

1. How did your life change after your baby was born?
2. What are some of the challenges you faced after having your baby?
3. Tell me about your transition from being a teen to being a teen mother.
4. Describe the feelings or emotions you experienced in your new role of being a mother.
5. What would you say was the most challenging part about being a teen mother, and how did you overcome the challenges?
6. Tell me about the positive experiences you have experienced since becoming a mother.

7. Describe a moment that made you feel proud about yourself as a mother.

After the interview, the researcher gave the participants time to ask additional questions or make any final remarks. The researcher also conducted a debriefing with each participant, explained the follow-up process, provided her with a list of resources and supportive counseling services, and informed her of follow-up that would take place after the data had been analyzed. After the interviews, the notes from the interviews were transcribed and analyzed for patterns and themes.

Data were analyzed using the Microsoft Excel program in the form of a spreadsheet. The researcher analyzed the transcripts by identifying natural meaning units. The results were displayed using descriptive analysis in a narrative format along with chart formats. Moustakas (1994) found that composite structural description represents the similar findings found within the total sample. Moustakas also suggested that researchers report individual structural descriptions for each participant.

Data Collection Processing and Analysis

The data analysis process consisted of the transcription of twelve interviews from twelve urban, adolescent mothers who shared their personal experiences and described their transition from being a teen to becoming a mother.

The phenomenological data analysis was adapted from the data analysis process used by Giorgi (1985, 2009), Stones (1979), and Moustakas (1994). The modified process consisted of analyzing and reviewing transcribed interviews, clustering and identifying natural meaning units, identifying the ideographic themes, and describing nomothetic themes presented in individual and composite structural descriptions.

In phenomenological research, the reported findings are presented as frequencies and percentages of identified themes. These themes are also usually presented in what Moustakas (1994) referred to as *individual structural descriptions* for each participant and a *composite structural description* for the group. Moustakas defined individual structural descriptions as providing a vivid depiction of the underlying dynamics of the experiences, themes, and qualities that account for how feelings and thoughts are connected with the phenomenon being studied (Wargo 2012). The identified structural descriptors were used as individual profiles, which included basic demographic information and a summary of each participant's experiences. Moustakas also asserted that the composite structural description is a way of understanding how the coresearchers (participants) as a group experience what they experience (p. 142). The structural descriptors were presented as a descriptive essay that summarized the collective experiences (the essence) for all participants in the context of each research question. The structural descriptors and themes were derived from the interview responses once the interviews were transcribed.

The face-to-face interviews were audiotaped and transcribed by the researcher. Data files were created and organized for each participant. The files were organized by the participant's order of interview, which served as an identifier. Reading and notations took place with the transcripts being read and initial natural meaning units identified. Bracketing was performed while analyzing the descriptions of personal experiences by natural meaning units, ideographic themes. The phenomenon was then identified by identifying the nomothetic themes. The classification of significant statements in the transcripts were identified and given codes. Similar statements made in the groups were coded and given meaning.

Repeated phrases and expressions were first identified and coded; these were termed the *natural meaning units* of each participant.

Stones (1979) defined natural meaning units as naturally occurring units with a particular meaning. The researcher reviewed the natural meaning units and eliminated the units that conveyed identical meanings (Stones 1979). The next step included the evaluation and reduction of the natural meaning units, which were then reviewed for relevance according to the phenomenon. The natural meaning units were compared with other natural meaning units to check for overlapping, repetitive, or vague expressions. These types of expressions were then eliminated, hence the reduction and elimination (Moustakas 1994).

The analysis process included identifying and clustering the natural meaning units. Reoccurring statements were first clustered and then compared with statements with the identified natural meaning units. The total the number of occurrences was then calculated. The natural meaning units were identified in each participant's transcript as the statements that were specific solely to that participant, after which the natural meaning units were assigned ideographic themes. The ideographic themes were more distinctive meanings given to the individual natural meaning units. The ideographic themes where then analyzed again, and the reoccurring themes were identified and clustered together. The synthesizing process began with the final identification of the nomothetic themes by application and validation. This process consisted of the identification of the reoccurring themes being clustered, labeled, and revaluated by an external auditor to whom the cluster themes were validated for their relevance.

The researcher conducted a data analysis (coding) of each of the first two participants' responses before continuing with subsequent interviews. This process enabled the researcher and the external evaluator to determine the quality of the interviewing process to identify possible leading comments or incomplete participant responses. This allowed for greater confidence and validity in conducting complete and accurate interviews. The researcher created a table using Microsoft Excel to code and analyze the data. After successful completion of the interviews, the researcher began transcribing the interview responses (Wargo 2012).

The researcher focused on improving the validity of the findings by using a *triangulation* method (Wargo 2012). Schwandt (2007) defined triangulation as a means of checking the integrity of the inferences one draws. It can involve the use of multiple data sources, multiple investigators, multiple theoretical perspectives, or multiple methods

(p. 298). Schwandt also noted that the strategy of triangulation is often wedded to the assumption that data from different sources or methods must necessarily converge or be aggregated to reveal the truth (p. 298). For the purpose of this research study and to increase validity, a three-step triangulation process adapted from Wargo (2012) was used.

The first step consisted of the interviews conducted and audiotaped. The second step was the transcription of audiotapes and the return of them to participants for their review and approval, which Wargo (2012) called *member check* (or validation). Wargo (2012) asserted that the practice of researchers submitting their data or findings to their informants (members) ensures that they correctly represent what their informants told them. This method is often used with data pertaining to interview summaries. The third and final step consisted of the researcher collaborating with an external auditor during data analysis (identifying meaning units from the transcripts and making the conversion into themes). The audit trail is considered a systematically maintained documentation system.

After successful completion of the triangulation process, data files were created that included filing, creating a computer database, and breaking large units into smaller ones (Creswell 1998). The classification process was the next step. This involved grouping the data into categories or themes and finding meaning in the data. Finally, the data were synthesized and used to offer hypotheses and the construction of tables, diagrams, and individual and composite structural descriptions.

Limitations of Research Design

Many standards and verification procedures are used when conducting qualitative research (Creswell 2007). Common critiques of qualitative research methodology consist of certain limiting conditions noted within this research study. Researcher subjectivity, participant reactivity, and transferability were all noted limitations of the study (Bloomberg and Volpe 2008; Creswell 2007). Researcher subjectivity is often a limitation to qualitative study, and the issue of researcher bias can affect the validity of the outcomes (Bloomberg and Volpe 2008; Merriam 2009). Another potential limitation of the study lies with *participant reactivity,* defined by Bloomberg and Volpe (2008) as interviewees having difficulty adjusting to the researcher taking on the role of interviewer. The participants may say what they believe the researcher wants them to say or what they think is the "correct response" without disclosing the truth. To avoid participant reactivity, the researcher made a conscious effort to create and establish a trusting and inviting interview session conducive to open dialogue. Also, the researcher ensured that the participant was informed of the confidentiality policy and that no judging would take place. The researcher also explained the significance of the study, which avoided any nonfactual information from being reported.

Restricting the sample population to urban adolescent mothers also limited the study, enabling it to be generalizable only to other similar groups of adolescent mothers. The researcher addressed the issue of generalizability through the use of transferability (Creswell 1998, 2007).

The lack of trustworthiness is a major threat and limitation in qualitative research (Creswell 1998, 2007; Patton 2002). It is a major factor in qualitative research and plays an important role in the researcher framing the interpretive paradigms (Lincoln and Guba 1985). Denzin and Lincoln (1994) suggested four factors to be considered when establishing trustworthiness in qualitative research: credibility, transferability, dependability, and conformability.

Creswell (2007) asserted that *validation* in qualitative research is the attempt to assess the accuracy of the findings described by the researcher and the participant (p. 207). To determine the validity of the data collection and the procedures, the researcher executed validation strategies suggested by Creswell and Miller (2000). Peer review or debriefing methods were executed, during which an individual provides an external check of the research process. The results from the field test revealed that the questions needed to use fewer academic words, and they needed to be more closely aligned with the research questions. A secondary review of the finalized research questions was completed, and the questions were deemed acceptable. The researcher held the peer debriefing sessions before beginning the research process. To ensure dependability of the study, the researcher used the same data collection procedures, analyses, and interpretation for the entire study. The consistency also included the use of audiotaping and verbatim transcripts of the interviews. Conformability was applied with the use of an audit trail, which included ongoing reflection and documentation of the findings (Lincoln and Guba 1998). These methods allowed the researcher to assess the final results and findings of the study.

Expected Findings

The primary goal of the phenomenological study was to obtain the essence of an experience (Merriam 2009). It was anticipated that the true meaning and essence of becoming a mother for urban adolescent mothers would be ascertained. It was also anticipated that the results would expand on the current research on the transitioning paradigms of urban adolescent mothers as they emotionally and perceptually transition from being teens to becoming mothers.

The outcomes of this study could be used to strengthen and expand on current programming provided by the researcher at a local state-licensed residential home to provide residential and community programming to adolescent mothers. The results could lead to further directions and details on how to effectively assist adolescent mothers both cognitively and emotionally as they transition into their new roles and develop dual identities.

Ethical Considerations

This population was considered to be vulnerable, and additional safeguards were taken to ensure that all ethical and human rights procedures were followed in accordance with the university Institutional Review Board (IRB), the Commonwealth of Virginia, and federal rules, regulations, and guidelines. Ethical concerns the researcher addressed included consent, confidentiality, privacy, and human rights considerations. Because of the potential vulnerability of the participants, the emotional state was a concern for the researcher. The researcher was concerned that the participants would have to relive past or current emotions they felt during their transition. Therefore, to avoid the risk of harm to themselves or their children after the interview, the researcher incorporated several safeguards.

First, the researcher screened the participants for eligibility criteria during the initial contact phone call. From the telephone call and the response to the screening questions, the researcher was able to determine whether the participant was a suitable candidate for the study and would not have any emotional turmoil or setbacks caused by disclosing or reliving the past. Second, during the interview process, the researcher had a state-licensed, professional counselor onsite during each participant's interview to ensure the availability of emotional assistance, if needed. Third, the researcher offered a list of resources and counseling services to the participants. The information regarding the additional assistance was given to the participants before and after they were interviewed, which provided them with additional resources for supportive services. The researcher reassured the participants during the screening—while reviewing the consent form and before beginning the interview—that they did not have to participate in the research study and that they had the option to leave the study at any time without penalty or repercussions (Beauchamp and Childress 2009).

1. After the interview, a debriefing period was held with the researcher to check the mental and emotional state of each participant after the interview.
2. The researcher called each of the participants one hour after the interview to check her emotional and mental state.
3. Before the start of the interview, names and contact information for two state-licensed mental health providers who offered free counseling services were provided. The licensed professional

counselor services were indefinite, and the licensed clinical social worker's services were limited to thirty days after the interviews were complete. Participants also received the number to a local crisis hotline.

Informed consent was addressed initially during the screening phone contact; the participants were told that to qualify, they had to be between the age of eighteen and twenty-two and have the ability to consent to the study. During the initial meeting for the interview, the participants were told to bring a state-issued identification card that displayed their date of birth (Beauchamp and Childress 2009). After the screening, the researcher provided a brief explanation and purpose of the study and disclosed the possibilities of risk, along with the inquiry of participation. Additional monitoring took place before the interview. The researcher reviewed the consent form orally with the participant to ensure her understanding of the research process. The potential candidate was also informed of the following safeguards of the study: researcher's credentials and expertise, licensed professional counselor being onsite during and after the interviews, debriefing of the licensed mental health provider and community service board clinical resources, and researcher's follow up phone call after the interview.

Confidentiality was addressed in detail with the participants before beginning the interview. A transcription of the interview was conducted by the researcher, and the data pertaining to the research was kept on a personal laptop and computer, which was double-password secured. All participants were given code names; only the researcher had the original list of names. All the demographic data pertaining to the research will be stored for a period of seven years on devices kept in a secure file cabinet located in the office of the researcher. After seven years, the data will be destroyed.

Summary

This chapter provided an overview of the methodological components used for this study. It provided distinct descriptions of the qualitative research methods and the rationale for the use of phenomenological research design used to capture the essence of the transitional process experienced by urban adolescent mothers as they evolved into becoming mothers. The chapter provided descriptions of the sampling process and formulated process for collecting data through in-depth, semistructured, face-to-face interviews. Data analysis procedures were demonstrated along with the descriptions of theoretical components of Erikson's psychosocial development theory, Kaiser and Hays's (2004) conceptual model, and Mercer's (2004) BAM theory, used to assist in analyzing and interpreting the data. The proposed study limitations, credibility, expected findings, and ethical concerns were all addressed in the chapter.

Chapter 4

FINDINGS

Introduction

The purpose of this phenomenological study was to provide a description of the experiences of twelve urban adolescent mothers as they transitioned into their roles as mothers. This study was important because the current research fails to recognize the effects early childbearing has on the psychosocial development of adolescents as they embrace their role of becoming a mother. This study gave credence to twelve urban adolescent mothers as they revealed their transitional experiences with various feelings, emotions, thoughts, and perceptions. Reliving their experiences through the data collection process enabled the researcher to uncover and provide the participants with a voice for their personal process and journeys they endured in discovering and developing their new role and identity of being a teen and becoming a mother. Moustakas (1994) contended that the increased clarification and expansion of meaning in a phenomenal experience as it is considered and reconsidered is known as *reflective processing*. The twelve participants engaged in their own reflective processes as they disclosed their experiences.

Through data collection of semistructured interviews, the researcher was able to bring understanding to the twelve participants' experiences and deem it as the knowledge of the participants' natural occurring units. Stone (1979) contended that the statements made by each participant are self-definable and self-delimiting in the expression of a single recognized experience.

The semistructured interviews were guided by the following research questions:

1. How do adolescent mothers develop maternal–role identity?
2. How do adolescent mothers describe the experience of transitioning from being a teen to becoming a teen mother?

This chapter presents the findings from the participants' interview responses. It also includes the descriptions of the participants' experiences, the data collection process, and the themes that emerged from the narrative descriptions. The process for the data collection included audiotaped interviews of twelve participants, transcription of the interviews, member checking to verify the transcripts, coding, categorization, and identification of the emergent themes.

The twelve adolescent mothers consented to be interviewed to discuss their transitions from being teens to becoming mothers. The participants were recruited from a local vocational center and daycare center theyhad been using. The interviews were also held either at the vocational center or the daycare center. Permission was granted from both locations, and a private office and classroom were used to conduct the interviews.

The interviews where scheduled for forty-five to sixty minutes. The semistructured interview consisted of seven questions pertaining to maternal-role identity and the transition to motherhood (Appendix D). The researcher used guided questions to ensure consistency and to make certain all questions were asked. All interviews where completed within the allotted sixty-minute timeframe, and additional time was used for the researcher to answer any questions. Three of the participants used the free counseling services available to them.

Description of the Sample

Recruitment

A Capella University IRB-approved recruitment flyer was given to two program directors of a local vocational program and a local daycare center known to have a high number of single adolescent mothers. Permission to post the flyers at the facilities was granted by the program directors after a meeting with the researcher. The flyers were posted in the open entrance areas of both facilities. They explained the purpose of the research, participation criteria, the required time commitment, and the possible benefits of the study. The participant requirement included being between the ages of eighteen and twenty-two, being the primary caretaker of the child, being a resident of the city where the study was taking place, and having a child between the ages of two months and thirty-six months. The participants also had to speak English and be able to comprehend and articulate past feelings and emotions regarding their transition to motherhood. The researcher's contact information was given for potential participants to call if they were interested.

After the initial phone call, a brief screening questionnaire was given to potential participants to ensure compliance with research criteria. Once the criteria were met, an interview was scheduled. The researcher met the participant at one of the approved locations in a private office, and she read and discussed the consent form with her. Once the consent form was signed, the researcher began the interview. --

Twelve adolescent mothers met the participation requirements, signed consent forms, and completed the interview. Three of the participants were interested in receiving the counseling services and resources available to them. Each participant revealed her transitional process from being a teen to becoming a mother and revealed her process of developing a maternal-role identity. Although each participant's transitional experience was individualized according to her personal accounts, reoccurring themes were highly prevalent throughout the course of the twelve interviews; therefore, at the conclusion of the interviews, saturation was met. Creswell (2009) contends that saturation is reached when the researcher no long finds new information that adds to the topic of discussion.

Demographics

The demographics of the sample population consisted of many variables that made the population so significant. The variation in the sample demographic supported findings of the study and led to implications for further research within this population. The demographics of the sample population consisted of single adolescent mothers, ranging in age from eighteen to twenty-two. There were ten African American women, one Caucasian woman, and one Native American/Pacific Islander woman, all of whom were residents of the city in which the study took place. The participants had a total of fourteen children; two moms had two children each. The ages of the children ranged from five months to thirty-six months. Eight of the teen mothers were high school graduates. Four participants had not graduated at the point of the interview; however, two were pursuing a graduate equivalent degree, and two were in their final year of high school. Eight of the participants were unemployed, and four had part-time jobs. At the time of the interview, only three of the participants had their own apartments; the remaining nine lived with a parent, relative, or friend. During the interview, seven of the participants mentioned lacking a stable home. Five of the participants were receiving assistance from a parent to take care of their children; the remaining seven were the sole providers for their children. Only three of the participants' children's father (or his family) actively assisted the participant with the child—either financially or supportively (physically or emotionally).

Data-Analysis Process

The phenomenological researcher attempts to bring to life the experiences of the individual participants through their descriptions (Moustakas 1994). Through data analysis, the researcher identified reoccurring themes that emerged from the analysis of the participants' shared experiences.

Data analysis consisted of the transcription and analysis of twelve interviews from twelve experiences and descriptions of their transitions from being teens to becoming mothers. The phenomenological data analysis consisted of the adaptation of data analysis processes (Giorgi 1985, 2009; Moustakas 1994; Stones 1979). The modified process involved analyzing and reviewing transcribed interviews for frequency of reoccurring descriptions; listing and preliminarily grouping the descriptions; reducing and eliminating overlapping, repetitive, and vague expressions; clustering and identifying natural meaning units; identifying the ideographic themes; and describing nomothetic themes.

The process began with the researcher first identifying and coding the repeated relevant expressions of natural meaning units of each participant, which Stones (1979) contended are naturally occurring units that have a particular meaning. After identifying the natural meaning units, the researcher reviewed them and eliminated those that had been repeated or that conveyed identical intention or meaning (Stones 1979).

The analysis process included identifying, clustering, and thematizing the natural meaning units. This involved clustering reoccurring meaning compared with natural meaning units and calculations of the number of occurrences to develop nomothetic themes. The natural meaning units were identified in each participant's transcript as the statements that were specific solely to that participant. After identifying the natural meaning units for each transcript, the natural meaning units were assigned ideographic themes. The ideographic themes were more distinctive meanings given to the individual natural meaning units. They established more collective meanings to the collected data. Ideographic themes were then analyzed again, and the reoccurring themes where identified and clustered. After the clustering of ideographic themes, the synthesizing process began with the final identification of the nomothetic themes by application and validation. This process consisted of the identification of the reoccurring themes being clustered, labeled, and revaluated by an external auditor to whom the cluster themes were validated for their relevance. The themes were considered valid if they were expressed explicitly in the transcript, were compatible if they were not expressed, or if they were relevant to the expressed experience. If not, they were deleted.

The emergence of relevant, validated nomothetic themes for each participant was summarized as an *individual structural description* of the experience, which also included verbatim examples of the meaning units. Participants individual phenomena were captured through their shared experiences to which the essence was captured in a reduced description (Creswell 2007).

The construction of the composite structural description consisted of a summary of experiences shared by all the participants. It concluded with the researcher identifying, labeling, and combining the participant's essence of her experience, incorporating the meaning units and nomothetic themes into a comprehensive summary of transitional experience into motherhood. Construction of the individual structural description and the composite structural description enabled the researcher to identify the true essences of the phenomenon the participants experienced (Moustakas 1994).

Findings

This study focused on the experiences of twelve urban adolescent mothers as they transitioned from being teens to becoming mothers and developing their maternal identities. The results identified six themes that emerged from the participants' responses: (a) experiencing conflicting identities, (b) defining a new and positive sense of self, (c) accepting maternal role duties and responsibilities, (d) constantly needing support, (e) experiencing emotional cycling, and (f) experiencing mental health symptomology. The results are presented both in tables and in a narrative format to include the individual textural and structural descriptions, composite textural description, a composite structural description, and a textual-structural synthesis that highlights the true essences of the phenomenon experienced by the twelve participants. The research identified relevant themes, categorized them according to degree of relevance to the research questions, and captured the essence of the phenomenon experienced for all twelve participants. Findings revealed common relevant responses that represent elements essential to the experience and perceptions of the individual participants and relevant to the research questions (Moustakas 1994). Within one hour of each interview, the researcher telephoned each participant. Overall results of the phone conversations consisted of the participants stating they were happy to have shared their stories and they were in good mood. They were glad the researcher listened, and they even felt excited, happy, and relieved—like a weight had been lifted off their chests; they felt like someone actually cared. Also, during the course of the interviews, the onsite licensed professional counselor was not used for any reason.

Individual Structural Descriptions

The purpose of the individual structural descriptions was to describe the vivid accounts of the underlying experiences as revealed by each of the twelve urban adolescent mothers as they transitioned into motherhood and developed their maternal identities.

According to Moustakas (1994), the individual structural descriptions account for the themes and qualities revealed through the feelings and thoughts of the experiences. In this case, experiences were shared. Twelve urban adolescent mothers revealed their emotions, feelings, and their process as they transitioned from being teens to becoming mothers and developing their maternal identities. The individual structural descriptions also included sample natural meaning units to bring clarity to the identified themes that emerged during this research (Table 1).

Table 1 – Shared Natural Meaning Units Expressed by Participants

Natural Meaning Units	P 1	P 2	P 3	P 4	P 5	P 6	P 7	P 8	P 9	P 10	P 11	P 12
Lost, unsure	x	x	x	x	x	x	x	x	x	x	x	x
Stressful	x		x		x	x	x		x	x	x	x
No support from child's father	x		x				x			x		
No support from others	x	x	x	x		x	x	x			x	x
Happy about being a mother	x	x	x	x	x	x	x		x	x	x	x
Unstable living environment	x	x				x	x	x			x	
Self-motivated to stay positive	x	x	x	x	x	x	x	x	x	x	x	
Became self-reliant/ independent	x		x	x	x		x	x	x		x	x
Realized actions affects her children	x	x	x	x	x	x	x		x			
Having a baby was positive change at the right time	x	x	x	x	x	x	x	x	x	x	x	x
School delayed		x	x		x	x				x		x
Puts child's needs first	X	x	x	x	x	x	x	x	x	x	x	x
Felt happy, sad, happy	x	x	x	x	x	x	x		x	x	x	x
Learned to think before acting	x	x	x	x	x	x	x	x	x	x	x	x
Experienced mental health symptomology	x	x	x		x	x	x	x	x	x	x	x

Participants

All participants are referred to by pseudonyms assigned by the researcher. This was done to protect their anonymity and confidentiality.

Tara, Participant 1

Tara was a twenty-year-old African American single mother with two children. She became pregnant with her first child when she was seventeen and a junior in high school. She became pregnant again with her second child one year later at the age of eighteen. She was a high school graduate, unemployed at the time of the interview, and had previously been in foster care. Tara was diagnosed with Bipolar I disorder and was taking medication for treatment. She described her family as not supportive; she met her biological mother and father for the first time when she was a teenager. During her transition, she experienced hurt and betrayal from her family because of their prejudgments about her and her high-risk lifestyle—and because of their lack of emotional and financial support. She had an estranged relationship with her biological mother. As an adult, Tara felt it was important for her to reach out to her mother to attempt to establish some sort of relationship. She appeared to resent her mother for not being around during her childhood and during her transition to being a mother herself.

She attributed her goal of trying to establish a relationship with her mother to having children of her own. Tara harbored bitter feelings toward her family because of their of lack of support during her pregnancy with her second child, which took a toll on her emotionally:

> When I thought, like, I wasn't doing the best that I can do or when I felt like I couldn't get the help from my family, I would break down because I felt

like nobody was on my side. I felt alone and, like, betrayed.

During this process, Tara learned to put her personal desires aside and concentrate and focus on her two children. She has received assistance from home visiting nurses and follows up with doctors who have a vested interest in her. These professionals also had concerns about her ability to care for her children. Tara shared that she was threatened several times that her children would be taken away from her if she did not change her priorities:

> To get myself to that point, it took me like two or three months, because after I had her, I wanted to party. There was an incident that happened at one party, and I was like, "I could've died." I wouldn't be here. And then I thought of my daughter. If I would've died, who would've took care of her? She would've been in the system. The kids' system and then another branch of the system—we don't need that.

The transition from being a teen to becoming a mother was very hard for Tara because of her lack of financial and emotional support. She also had to learn to share herself with others. Because she had an unstable living environment as a child (living with various relatives and in foster care), it was hard for Tara to establish her own home environment. She found herself and her children without stable living environments, moving around a lot and not having a home of their own:

> And like I said, I was a little bit lost. I was so lost I was running from my problems, like I was moving from north side to the east end, to the south side, everywhere. I moved around a lot, and my kids, they lost a lot of stuff.

Tara struggled with maintaining her mental health disorder and attempting to take care of her two children alone. She spoke of feeling lost, betrayed, hopeless, angry, sad—but also sometimes happy—when her children were around. She spoke about learning to manage her disorder and learning not to let her emotions or feelings get the best of her, definitely not in front of her children:

> And I know that's not good, and sometimes I find myself ready to snap, and I have to remember I can't, because you know I have to think about my kids and how they feel with me going off. So I don't want to go off 'round them. I senthem away so they won't think, *Momma going crazy*.

Tara shared her stories of self-reflection, determination, and perseverance. She had experiences of letdowns, betrayals, and eventual support; however, she remained determined to be a good mother to her two children. She explained she did not know her biological mother or father until she was a teenager, and she felt it was important to know and understand what it was like to be a part of a family. She did feel the pain and anguish of not having a mother growing up when she battled the task of becoming a mother herself; she did not have a natural guide to model or direct her. She reflected on this by stating,

> But it's like I went through so much, you know, messed up shit as a child—I didn't want my children to go through and felt what I felt with. It was a lot I dealt with, and I dealt with it.

When asked about a time when she felt proud to be a mother, she replied:

> When I realized that I knew that I had to do the right thing, because I didn't have my mom. So you know

automatically when you don't have your mom you're going to be the best mom that you can be.

Tara stated that it was hard to give up her high-risk and partying life style for her children, but she felt it was the best thing that had happened to her. She spoke about the hard times, but knowing she had two children that love her unconditionally helped her weather her depressive moods, manic attacks, and negativity fueled by disappointment and disgust spewed by her family members.

> I didn't even have support from some of my family, because they thought, *Oh, I was too young and pregnant*, and I didn't have a stable house and a home for my kids so I shouldn't have my kids, or would I have them, or I should give them up for adoption because of my life. They didn't think that my life was right for my children.

Tara remained resilient through all the negative perceptions and comments by family members. Through self-determination and motivation, she maintained custody of her two children, established a stable living environment, maintained her mental health diagnosis with her medication, and had hopes of finding employment. She used the negative comments to persevere. Tara stated she was not ready to be a mother at either time during her teenage life; however, she did not think her life would have been in a positive state at that point if she had not had them. Having her children made her calm down and think twice before acting, and it motivated her to want to do positive things. Her children were a positive inspiration to her and had a positive effect on her life. This was revealed when she stated, "I keep … I think like every day if I didn't have my childrens, where would I be?"

The Essence of Tara's Experience

Tara struggled with accepting her role of being a mother because of her current cognitive state in which she wanted to remain a teenager. She had constant turbulent times, including lack of support, poor perceptions from others, negative comments, feelings of self-doubt, and an unstable living environment. However, through all of the turbulence of finding stable housing, lacking support, and dealing with mental health issues, Tara developed a sense of empowerment and resilience. She found solace in herself and reached out to develop a relationship with her biological mother. This inspired her to be a better mother to her children than her mother was to her. Tara recognized and accepted that she was a mother and was determined to continue to strive to be a good mother.

Mia, Participant 2

Mia was a Caucasian single mother age nineteen with an eighteen-month-old son. She became pregnant when she was seventeen during her junior year in high school. Her boyfriend, her child's father, was a senior and was able to graduate from high school. However, Mia's high school graduation plans were placed on hold for months during her pregnancy and after having her son. She did graduate from high school and at the time of the study was in the process of enrolling in community college. She was unemployed at the time of the interview. Mia and her boyfriend both lived with her family when she was pregnant. She described him as being as very supportive throughout the entire transition. She stated, "My boyfriend is very supportive to me and our son. He was there through it all from pregnancy to being a mom (*laugh*) a dad." Mia described her family as not supportive and as dysfunctional, with the exception of her mother. Even with them all living in one home, they never provided her with support. While pregnant, she wanted to obtain her own housing for herself, her child, and her boyfriend. At the time of the interview, Mia and her boyfriend were still living with her family. Mia described her boyfriend and her mother as supportive throughout her transitional process:

> Like, we live with my family, and my boyfriend or me may get our own place soon, so I think that would be a lot more stress-free. It is hard living with a lot people and not havin' a lot of people living together in one home and no one really helping out.

Mia was asked about the help she received from her boyfriend in her transition to being a mother. She replied,

> He's taking care of us. He was there to support me. Even when other people did not, he was there. He encourages me in positive ways and supports me on my decisions and is a part of my life. Yeah, because with teens that is not normal, most dudes are one from the jump. He was there when I was going [through] the ten thousand emotions I was experiencing.

Mia described her transition as an experience filled with a lot of mixed emotions. She explained that her emotions fluctuated often—from angry to sad to happy—and those emotions caused her to worry about her baby's well-being. She appeared to have conquered some of her fears and emotions by thinking of her baby's needs, planning, thinking about the future, and remaining goal-oriented:

> I didn't really, you know, I didn't know what I was going to do first. Not like keeping it or not, you know, if me and boyfriend's going to work out. I think long term: Where am I going to be?

> What am I going to be doing? Will I be able to graduate high school?

Mia described her transitional experience as emotional, and she had a hard time explaining the feelings she felt during that time in her life:

> It was pretty emotional. I guess you, like … I guess you could say, 'cause like, I don't know. Yeah, it was just pretty emotional. I don't know the words to explain it. I keep trying to not worry about everything, like where to live and taking care of my baby. Just trying to stay focused and not let life get ya' down was hard to do. We're kind of struggling.

She also mentioned she did not endure a great deal of stress during this transitional period in her life. She did, however, say that she wondered how she would face challenges of time management and balancing her schoolwork, the baby's needs, and taking care of herself:

> Challenges … challenges … none really, I guess I would find out like more what's going to happen later on, like whether, like if I was going to start school in August, like then how I could I breastfeed, so … maybe some of my time would be challenging for me to balance it. So I guess, like I said, trying to go to school.

Mia did appear to find solace by recognizing that even though she did not change as a person after having the baby, she was happy with deciding to keep her baby. She recognized her thought process had to change. She mentioned she was glad she was not like "other teen mothers," whose boyfriends were not around to help them through the transition or assist them with taking care of their babies. She recognized her boyfriend was an integral part of her life, played a significant role in assisting her during her transition, and provided the support she needed.

It was a little stressful, but like, it's—you know, I made it work. I had to get myself together, had to be ready. I'm not me anymore. I didn't really become somebody different. I just … I never thought it would happen to me. I mean, I knew eventually I would be a mom, but not this soon. But, um, when I was with my son, I didn't feel left out or anything. Nothing really changed that much for me anyway. Because if you lay on your back, you know you have to pay—there's consequences. I didn't really become somebody different. I just … I never thought it would happen to me. I mean, I knew eventually it would.

Even though Mia admitted that she would have liked to have had her son later on, she had no regrets for her early childbearing. Her son appeared to have provided her with a sense of hope and well-being and served as a positive light in lieu of her dysfunctional family and the unsupportive environment in her mother's household. She found peace and comfort in her son's presence. When she was asked about any other good moments experienced during the transition she replied,

Nawh, I love being a mom. I guess just looking at him and when he smiles, it just changes—your heart melts completely. You can have your worst day ever and just look, like, at your child, and it changes it … it makes it all better.

The Essence of Mia's Experience

Mia accepted her role and responsibilities of being a mother. She recognized that having her child's father with her was very beneficial to her and helped her avoid the high level of stress that is often experienced by adolescent mothers. Mia also recognized the sacrifice motherhood entails, and she has made them without any questions or doubts. Her life is now about providing for her son.

Ariel, Participant 3

Ariel was a nineteen-year-old African American single mother with a two-year-old son. Ariel become pregnant her junior year of high school and had her son in her senior year. She graduated from high school and at the time of the interview had a job working at a local fast food restaurant. Ariel disclosed that her mother walked out of her life when she was younger. She was raised by her biological father with her grandmother's assistance. Ariel suffered from severe mood swings and stated she was often depressed during her transition. She did not receive medical treatment for her depression; nor did she seek any therapeutic services for her symptoms of depression that occurred daily. After the interview, Ariel mentioned that Bipolar disorder runs in her family, and she felt she had it. Ariel described her biological father as being very supportive of her during her transition and a person she relied on heavily; however, he was battling alcoholism. Ariel explained that her transition was full of many emotions and was very taxing on her; having the baby made her change her behavior. During the interview, she recounted her experience. "I had to sacrifice so much, like high school," she said. "I had to stop going to school. And I stopped hanging out with friends. And I grew up too fast and that changed me!" She was then asked about the things that made her grow up too fast:

> Being a mom. I was being tied down. I got to work. Being tired. When I thought like I wasn't doing the best that I can do or when I felt like I couldn't get the help from my family, I would break down because I felt like nobody was on my side. I felt alone and, like, betrayed.

Ariel faced a lot of challenges during her transition: having no income, depending on others for support who didn't seem reliable to her, and most of all enduring this process by herself. Her son's father was very inconsistent with his support, which made her experience filled with stress and resentment. When Ariel was asked about a challenge she endured during the transition, she responded:

> The dad not being around. I mean, he just left out with us. He was there one minute, and now he's gone. I do that all by myself, raise him … and he ask me about his daddy and what am I supposed to say?"

Living was a challenge for Ariel. During the interview, her eyes begin to fill up with tears, and her entire disposition changed from being sad to becoming angry. Her feelings were evident from the changes in her tone of voice and facial expressions.

> Like, we had to have help with everything because we had to depend on other people for things, and that gets irritating 'cause people are fake and help one minute and tell you no the next. When you [don't] work they be like, "Get a job …" When you get a job they like, "Watch your baby; go to school."
>
> I'm like, how am I going to pay for everything? Having a baby is not, you know, easy. It takes a lot of patience. You got to have an income.

Ariel experienced multiple mood swings, and she questioned individuals' sincerity in assisting her. The lack of consistency from her son's father and her family members caused her additional anguish. She did, however, recognize after having the baby that it was time for her to "grow up" and become more mature.

I had to grow up. No more hanging out late at night. I had to bite the bullet and stop doing all the wild stuff I was doing—partying, hanging out late, doing whatever whenever, drinking, smoking, going out to chill with friends—all that had to stop! I was like, "Nawwhh, I want my life back." I don't want that. It was hard. You're always so tired. They tell you to sleep when the baby's sleeping, but once you're up, you can't go back to sleep. Yeah, I'd get grumpy. Everybody was like aggravating.

Ariel's moods did not appear to affect her understanding of her role as a mother. She had to learn how to deal with herself and her own mood swings to be able to deal with her son's daily needs. She was able to use her son's birth and her current situation as a source of positive reinforcement to help motivate her during trying times. Ariel's moods fluctuated day to day, and it took a lot of inner personal strength to remain positive and accept her role as a mother.

I had my days where I'd, you know, I'd be right there with him. I could be happy about it. Other days are my, like, down days, when I'm like, *man*. My down days, like, depending on how it was, like if I woke up in a bad mood, I stayed in a bad mood all day. But some days would be better. It was hard to find good motivation. It was hard. I just didn't like anybody, and people stop being around me, because I always had an attitude. My baby made me mad, but he made me smile; seeing his face and him spitting for no reason made me laugh all the time. I guess you can say that was the motivation, because people around me brought me down all the time.

Ariel described her down days as terrible. She stated, "It's like I didn't want nobody around me. I really didn't want to be bothered with him sometimes. Just tired and stressed out." She stated that her stressor was being a single parent and not having help that she felt she should have.

Ariel's role transformation was engulfed by a lot of mixed emotions and feelings. She felt the brunt of the duties and responsibilities of being a single mother, but she also had to endure the fact that her teenage days were numbered. She could not do what she wanted all the time, because she could not fulfill both duties at the same time—being a teen and being a mother. When asked about overcoming the challenges of being a teen mother, she said:

> Being with my son, watching him grow up, actually growing up with him [was a challenge]. Not, you know, I'm always working. It was being at home with him that was challenging because I was bored. I missed my friends. You know, it's hard to be a teen and a mom. Yeah. Some of my friends will be going late at night, and I'd be at home with a baby.

Ariel described how she felt when she realized she had to forfeit many of her normal teenage social activities. She was upset with her child's father because she felt it was unfair for her to be the only one sacrificing for their son. When asked how she felt, she answered, "Mad! Because it's like, why should I get to be tied down while his dad's out there, you know, partying with my friends, and I'm stuck at home!"

Even though Ariel had moments during her transitional period, she was able to conceptualize her son as a symbol of positivity and love. Even though she spoke about the negative perceptions and thoughts that others had formulated about her, she always viewed her son as her personal "sunshine." Having this perception kept her focused and motivated to uphold her role as a mother and embrace her newfound identity. She still was encumbered with thoughts of having to raise her son on her own with little to no support from her son's father and minimal support from family members, except her own father. However, she was able to persevere and attempted to make changes in her life that benefited her son.

> Learning how to be positive, 'cause once you start getting used to it, you don't look back and think about the bad things so much … just stay positive and motivated, I guess. You just keep going. Watching him, like, you know, hearing him wake up every morning, getting dressed, seeing his smile. Him saying, "Mommy."

Ariel was determined to be there for her baby and to model positive maternal characteristics to her son, because she had to endure her childhood with an absent mother. She was resilient in the thought that because her mother was not there for her, she would be diligent in being there for *her* child, emotionally and physically. When speaking about her absent mother and the role of motherhood, Ariel's voice inflection changed and she spoke slower and in a lower tone.

However, she pulled herself up to discuss the positive and opposite things she does with her son in lieu of her mother's indiscretions. The researcher asked a question about any other positive experiences since becoming a mother. Ariel replied, "Becoming a better mom than what my mom was. Not leaving my child.

She wasn't always around." Ariel was asked what things she did differently at this point, and she responded without hesitation, "I didn't give my kid up. I'm always there for my son. Like that is mad positive compared to my life without my mom; I am there every day for my baby!"

The Essence of Ariel's Experience

During Ariel's transformation from being a teen and adjusting to her role as a mother, she appeared to have developed a sense of advocacy for herself.

This was apparent in her responses to questions when she spoke about people not being there for her or putting her down for being a teen mother. Granted, she did not like the situations she often found herself in, but she still motivated herself to move forward and stay positive. She described many emotions of pain, abandonment, and fear, but she maintained her status that she was going to be a better mother than her mother was to her. When the researcher asked her if she had any last words she wanted to share about her transition to motherhood that were not said during the interview, she replied,

> Yes. I think teen moms need to be positive and not give up and not [let] people get us down and mad. Just know that we are somebody and we make mistakes, but my baby wasn't a mistake. I mean, I love him to death, wasn't ready for him, but I may be positive and not somebody negative that somebody to like bring you down. Because people think you bad or ruin your life when you have a baby early, and that is not true, and they always trying to bring you down. You know, talk about you and roll their eyes when they see you walking with your baby. I hated that. I finished school and have a job, and I am not a loser or lost cause. You can't judge the way they raise it, because, you know, you probably work as hard as they do with their children. You want to know, like, different … every child is different.

The researcher asked Ariel what she liked about being a mother. She replied with a big smile, "Seeing my son and kissing him every day!"

Shay, Participant 4

Shay was a nineteen-year-old African American single mother with a one-year-old daughter. She became pregnant her junior year of high school but was able to graduate with her diploma on time. Shay's experience was that she had the financial, emotional, and physical support of both her mother and her father, with whom she lived at the time of the study. Not only was Shay able to complete her high school diploma, but also she was able to obtain a state license to be a Certified Nursing Assistant (CAN) and was able to obtain employment with that certification. At the time of the interview, Shay had a full-time job, lived at home with her parents, and was enrolled full time in community college.

Shay spoke about her pregnancy and transitional process with a big smile and with an upbeat mood She began the interview raving about how thankful she was for the emotional support her mother offered her. She shared that at first she was scared and nervous to tell her parents she was pregnant, because she did not want to disappoint them or other family members. However, after she shared her situation with them, they were onboard with her having the baby and helped her through her entire transition. Shay's major disappointment about her early childbearing situation was the response of her child's father to her pregnancy. She was very upset with his lack of commitment and involvement he had throughout her pregnancy and the birth of their daughter.

> Well, I was in still in school. And I like school, and then having her, having to come home and take care of her and working. So and she was, like, a baby, baby. That was a lot too. But I mean, I had a lot of help, so I was—I was never really stressed. And family, like, I have a really good family, so we were all there!

As with the other participants, Shay still experienced the emotional effects of transitioning into motherhood as an adolescent. Shay spoke about her emotional bouts of crying for two days straight when she brought her daughter home from the hospital and she was feeling uncertain. She had to struggle with the feeling of uncertainty and wondering whether she would be able to properly care for her daughter. She had to find the inner strength to be a good mother.

Shay shared that—with help from her mother and father—she was able to get the hang of parenting and that she ultimately discovered a sense of independence. She said her level of anxiety was reduced shortly after she gained the necessary confidence to parent her daughter.

Shay began to develop her maternal-role identity by recognizing that her entire concept of thinking began to change. This was evident by the decisions she began to make when it came to going out with her friends.

> Like, I couldn't just pick up and go when friends called, like, I was like, oh, well, let me see if I have a babysitter, or it was like—sometimes it was like, no, I'm not going to go, because I'm not going to always leave her, and that's how it is now; like no, I won't go, because I'm not going to leave her. Plus, now that she's at that age where she knows if I'm there or not, so ...

Shay said she felt happy, nervous, and excited during her transition to motherhood. When asked what made her happy, she explained that she was glad she went through the process of having her child and not getting an abortion, which was what her boyfriend (at the time) wanted her to do. Her mother convinced her to have her baby, and she remarked several times she was glad she listened to her mother.

> Just happy that, like, I don't know, just happy that I went through with it, just having her altogether, because like, between like my feelings and her dad's feelings, they were totally different. So it's like, I was glad I stuck with my decision instead of going with the easy way out. When I thought about it, and after

I told my mom, she was like, "You're not getting no abortion. We're going to help you!"

Shay reported that her biggest stressor was the feeling of abandonment from her boyfriend, because she really wished he had been around during and after her pregnancy to help her. Even though other family member constantly told her he would come around, at the time of the interview he still had not. She expressed sadness about the situation because she wondered how having an absent father would affect her daughter.

Shay knew what it felt like to have a supportive father because of her own father's support during this transitional phase of motherhood.

Her dad. Dealing with him was horrible. I wish he would have helped. Just helping me with, like, getting ready to have her and being there, just being there. Um, they (my parents) helped me through school, which was, you know, that was a big thing because I got my CNA. And so that was, like, another big thing. They helped me, like, prepare for, you know, moneywise.

Shay spoke of the positive experiences she had engaged in during her transition to motherhood. A key thing she learned was how to be more responsible. She stated she had to change her way of thinking and begin to put her daughter's needs first. She felt becoming more responsible was an important element for her, because previously she would always lose her personal items.

I had to learn to be—just to be more responsible. That, and you know, just that, by itself, just because, like, my mom would always tell me, you are so irresponsible … you know, because I would, like, lose my phone and stuff like that. And she [her mother] would always tell me, like, when me and her—when it was just me and her, and you left, she would be, like, don't you forget that baby in the backseat. So, like, it was like, I had to be more responsible. I had to remember, like, I have, you know, somebody else, and not just me. I never—even if she was quiet—I never forgot that she was back there.

Shay embraced and accepted her role as a mother. She also recognized key behaviors she needed to change, and she did so without hesitation. She used the support and assistance she had from her mother and father and other family members and made choices that were beneficial to her daughter.

She said that her role model for being a good mother was her own mother.

I knew, you know, like, what I had to do in order to be, you know, a good mom or try to be a good mom. It just came naturally. It came natural because I didn't try to fight it! I wanted to share myself and life with my baby. Some girls don't want to give that up. I didn't have any problems with it.

The Essence of Shay's Experience

Having her daughter made Shay grow up and mature. She stopped putting her needs and desires first and began to look out for her daughter. Shay embraced her role of being a mother and appeared to appreciate the adults around her who provided her nurturance, support, and guidance. Shay was happy with the mature changes she made in life, and others around her noticed it as well.

Tina, Participant 5

Tina was a nineteen-year-old Native American/Pacific Islander single mother with a five-month-old daughter. She became pregnant during a time in her life when she did not have a stable home environment. She was seventeen and had been living on the streets with friends. She was asked to leave her mother's home because of her noncompliance with her mother's rules and her gang member affiliations. Tina lived various places with different people, and during that period she became pregnant. At the time of the interview, she had started to live with her mother again. Tina was unemployed. She had dropped out of school in the eighth grade and had refused to go to school again. She anticipated starting a GED program once she became more stabilized and found her own housing and employment. She had minimal to no support raising her daughter. Her child's father was one of her male friends in the gang she had left. He offered her verbal parenting advice but no financial support in taking care of their daughter. Her mother had minimal means and was struggling herself, but she assisted Tina when she could. Tina shared that one of the positive benefits of having her baby was that it reunited her with her mother. They began to work on rekindling their relationship.

Tina endured a great deal of emotional turmoil and personal growth during her transition from teen to mother. She felt she had a daughter at the right time in her life because of her previous lifestyle. She was homeless, a gang member, and did various street drugs. She had a violent temper, was easily provoked, and experienced a high level of anxiety. She also felt that having her daughter helped her grow as an individual and become a better person; the experience gave her solidarity and strength. Tina spoke about the strong emotions she endured during her transition to motherhood. The majority of her responses were about the feelings she endured after her daughter's birth. A high level of anxiety was the first emotion she felt when daughter was born. Dealing with her anxiety required her to engage in self-regulation and evaluation to determine how she would handle the anxiety.

> My anxiety level has been up since I've had a child. As in, when I didn't have a child, I had no way to cope with things, but now, since I have a child, my answer is totally different because my anxiety is much higher now. I can't really explain it. I mean, it's just high, you know.

Tina also experienced a great deal of anger and frustration while she transitioned into her new role of being a mother. She had a difficult time dealing with the emotional needs of her child because of her level of uncertainty and lack of self-confidence at the time. When she discussed her emotions and feelings, she shook her head, wrung her hands, and slapped her fist in her hand as if she was reliving the situation.

> I get very angry. Very angry, very frustrated, and very agitated. That's most definitely, now since I've had a child. Well, when I ... when I ... when my child is, like, you know, crying or screaming or needs something, then I get very frustrated, and I get angry, and then ... anything like that at that moment will set me off.

Tina expressed how having her daughter gave her a sense of personal enlightenment and how it provided her a sense of accomplishment and gave her a voice. She was able to cope with the personal enhancement she felt when she became a mother; however, she struggled with the maternal and emotional responsibilities. When Tina was not frustrated with her newfound responsibilities and challenges, she often worried about her own capabilities and the well-being of her daughter. She stressed over battling with herself to do the right thing for her daughter. With Tina's previous malicious background of gang activity, violence, and drugs, she fought to remain focused and not get stressed out so as not to handle her stress with her previous self-destructive behaviors.

> My stress level has definitely been higher since I've had a child, also. I stress out a lot more about my needs, her needs—you know, what's important, what's not important. Stuff that is sometimes irrelevant, I stress out about that, stuff like that, so I do stress out a lot more now. I mean, I don't ... like, my thoughts on it, like, I just know I stress out a lot. My thoughts on it, like I need to stop stressing out so much. Just for the benefit of her, but you know, it is what it is.

Tina managed to embrace her role as mother through the encouragement of her daughter's life.

Even though she lacked the necessary support at times, her daughter's presence in her life was a spark of positivity. Tina spoke about her daughter's life, which gave her a voice and the self-confidence she lacked. When she was asked about her transition from being a teen to becoming a mother, she replied:

> Oh, yes, most definitely it was a transition for me. After having her, I changed—got a voice. I'm more confident in myself. I feel like that because I'm responsible for a human being now. You know, like, I'm responsible for a child. So I feel more confident and more determined. Compared to what I used to be in myself, I wasn't that confident in myself. I felt like I couldn't get nothing done. I felt like, you know, everything was, everything was just unimportant to me, basically. Not important at all. Now I feel, like I said, confident and determined to get everything done now. Because of her!

Tina discussed the fact she had to seek treatment from a therapist to assist her with her emotions and postpartum depression. She shared that postpartum depression took a toll on her thought process, and she was very emotional. One characteristic that stood out about Tina was that she took initiative to seek help, whether it was from a therapist, other individuals, or even reading books. She did not allow ignorance to be a barrier for her lack of knowledge and skill set. That approach appeared to at least keep her grounded as she continued to try to do the right things for her daughter. When she was asked how she dealt with her postpartum depression, she responded, "Anything that I let stay in my mind, [I] let it get to me, that's mostly that, and me being happy is because of her; the depression was because it was something new to me being a mom."

Tina was still resilient and was able to manage her postpartum depression and care for her baby.

She described what she went through:

> It was sad, mostly, you know, because I was sad, confused, stuff like that because, you know, this is something new—like, you know, you have to learn to deal with it and know when it is coming on. I went to therapy and got some pills.

Tina was able to use her inner strength and confidence to learn patience, which was a key factor for her. She said, "Learning patience was a positive experience for me." Learning patience helped her continue to see the value in her daughter even during the times she became frustrated with her.

> Every moment is wonderful with her. Having her was a proud moment. I changed because of my daughter, and I just love being a mom, you know. Just the fact of, she's mine. You know, she's my flesh; she's my blood. She's with me 24–7. And having her, I changed a lot.

Tina's life changed because of her daughter, and she embraced her newfound role from being a "party animal" and doing drugs to becoming a mother. She recognized that the changes in her life were for the betterment of her own well-being.

> Now, being a mom has changed me a lot. You have to … I've calmed down a lot. From being a party animal to being a mom, you know, basically. You know, I used to think that there was nothing out here for me—you know, that I was going to be nobody, but now, you know, seeing her, looking at her every day, you know, you're doing something for a reason.

The Essence of Tina's Experience

Tina went through several transformations as she endured the pathway of motherhood. She found self-empowerment, perseverance, and inner personal strength to overcome a violent and drug-induced life style. Tina recognized she could no longer be involved in a gang-member life style; she had someone to live for, and someone needed her. Tina looked at her pregnancy as a blessing and something positive that she needed to become a better person and mother.

Lynn, Participant 6

Lynn was a twenty-one-year-old African American single mother with a ten-month-old daughter. Lynn was a high school graduate and at the time of the interview was in the process of enrolling in a two-year college. Lynn was unemployed and currently receiving a disability social security check. Lynn mentioned she suffered from postpartum depression and Bipolar I disorder, for which she takes medication. Lynn stated she had a large family but that they provided little support to her for her daughter. She had recently moved into her own apartment after living with her daughter's father. He was arrested for selling drugs, and his home had to be evacuated. Her daughter's father had been incarcerated and offered her no assistance in providing for their daughter. His incarceration left her without a place to live, and she had to move in with various friends and family members for about two months. Lynn discussed her transformation from being a "wild child" to becoming a mother and how having a baby changed her entire outlook on life:

> Well, I think I matured a lot. Um, it had to change my whole view of my whole outlook of things. My personality, like, it kind of changed because I kind of, like, think some things more through than I do other things.

Lynn's conversations focused on her transition as a new learning experience for her physically and mentally. She spoke about changes she made in her thought process and decision-making, both concerning the well-being of her daughter and a better outlook for herself. Lynn took on the experience of her transition head on and paid attention to the possible outcomes.

> I would also say I become more confident, 'cause it's hard being a mom, but then at the same time, it depends on how you do it. Like someone told me, that a baby can make you or break you. It depends which, how you, which way you go!

Lynn also recognized that the existence of her daughter made her want to strive to be more and to be a better person. With her perseverance and ongoing motivation, she made decisions that in the past she wouldn't have given any thought to,

> I feel like she [my daughter] made me because she made me go the extra mile to do more things that I probably wouldn't even want—like, I started school but I dropped out and really didn't care, but now I'm

back in school and I know it, that I have to finish school.

Lynn also had many challenges to overcome during her transition to motherhood. She stated she had no help from her daughter's father or her family. She also struggled because she did not have a stable living environment to call home. Lynn said, "I needed a better support system, because maybe I wouldn't have went through all the things that I went through if I had a better support system—that was a big problem for me and my baby." Not having a stable environment and lacking a support system created a stressful living situation for Lynn. She felt herself stressing daily about finding the means to take care of her daughter, and not having a stable place to live contributed to her severe postpartum depression, which she endured after having her daughter.

> My postpartum was bad and caused me a lot of problems. I had no place to live, no, always stressed me out and worrying and no one helped me, which pissed me off even more!

Lynn took medication to help her control and manage her postpartum depression. She sought support with a psychiatrist and said, "Pills, I mean I went to a psychiatrist and some medication for my depression and anxiety." Lynn also spoke about her high levels of anxiety and stress, but she also had to endure negative comments and perceptions from the people she lived with.

The reactions from her family to her pregnancy affected Lynn's transition because she experienced a great deal of negative thinking. While she tried to embrace her new role as a mother and feel good about herself, she endured the negative remarks from those around her from family and friends. She also noticed that some friends stopped coming around after she had her baby. Lynn said she was stressed because she felt that many of her family members and friends were disappointed in her for having her baby.

> What people thought, what they said, how people
> acted toward me. Like really not wanting to be
> involved—like some of my friends said before I was
> pregnant, some of them are not my friends now,
> because I have a baby, and I guess they feel I can't do
> the same things that they do now—which, I still have
> a life; I still can do stuff, but I guess they feel like I
> can't do toward me.

Lynn experienced many different feelings and emotions during her transition. In addition to feeling high levels of anxiety and stress, she questioned her ability to parent

> My anxiety was really high. I was nervous a lot. I
> didn't know if I was going to be able to be a mother.
> I still thought I was a child myself, and I didn't know
> how to take care of a baby. I didn't even know how
> to make a bottle, so it was very, very hard for me. I
> was very scared.

Lynn had to overcome the challenge of learning how to be a mother. She lost her own mother at a young age, and she had to learn how to become a mother on her own.

> I had to teach me how to be a mom since my mom
> passed away. I learned that no mom is a better mom,
> and there's just different techniques that everybody
> uses for different ways to raise their child. I had to
> learn a lot on my own.

She had to learn how to manage her stress, and she had to gain a sense of patience while parenting her daughter; she found this beneficial not only to her but also to her daughter. In reference to her learning about patience, she said, "I didn't have any patience before having my baby, and I had to teach myself to have more patience because she don't understand." Lynn rationalized with herself that her daughter had needs, and she had to learn to accept that. Lynn found positivity in herself as she endured her path to motherhood on her own. She revealed she had great self-reflection and self-endurance and tried to be the best mother she knew how to be. She was grateful for her daughter coming into her life; it helped her change her high-risk living ways.

> I love being a mom. I love it. I just love our relationship. I love having someone that loves me as much as I love them. I did some wild, crazy things. Like, there were a lot of things that I would do … you know … when I was younger, but I probably wouldn't do now and that makes me proud. I used to pop pills and ride down the street and hold the horn, or go to the club, just to see how many people I could fight, get expelled from school just because I didn't feel like going to school. There was stuff like that that I wouldn't do today, because I'll be thinking about my baby.

The Essence of Lynn's Experience

Lynn's daughter was the pinnacle of positivity for her. She was the one thing that made Lynn's attitude, behavior, and ways of living change for the better toward self-preservation. Although Lynn lived a high-risk lifestyle, her thoughts became more positive and she was filled with compassion for her daughter. Perseverance and resilience resounded around her when others reminded her of her "old self." Lynn was determined to prove to the naysayers that she was capable of caring for a loved one. She recognized she had her own demons, and she had to deal with them for the welfare of herself and her daughter. She was willing to do all it took to accomplish that.

Jackie, Participant 7

Jackie was a twenty-one-year-old African American single mother with two children. She became pregnant with her first child when she was fifteen years old and an eighth grader in junior high school. She was nineteen when she became pregnant with her second child. Jackie graduated from high school and had recently been enrolled full time at a community college. At the time of the interview, she was taking a break from her courses to concentrate on finding a job.

Jackie disclosed she had been in foster care for two years and had been raised by her grandmother, who passed away when she was twelve. After her grandmother died, Jackie went to live with her father, but he was very unstable and suffered from drug and alcohol abuse. Jackie also disclosed that she did not grow up with her mother, who lived in another state. She said she had to take care of herself and her father while learning how to be a mother throughout her high school and young adult years. Jackie's life changed drastically after having a child. She dealt with ongoing homelessness, living with different people for months at a time, unemployment—plus having to take care of family members, her children, and herself.

> It was just, I panicked a whole lot … because it was like I was under the age of twenty-one with two children already. When I did have her, I was going through some things as far as my living situation was concerned … that I lost my own apartment. I just had to put everything in—I just had to put everything in order, you know, just to get everything together to make sure they didn't have a life like [I] had.

Jackie suffered from depression but never received treatment. She described her transitional process as very stressful and depressing. Jackie's depressive symptoms took such a toll on her emotionally and physically that some days she couldn't get out of bed. Jackie also disclosed that she handled her stressful life situations at times with the use of crack cocaine.

> I was so depressed ... never had the time to go see a counselor or see a therapist or see a psychiatrist or anything like that, but I was always, like, crying, worried; it hurt or whatnot, so I went through a lot of like physical changes ... Just had a lot of migraine headaches. Sometimes I don't want to get out of bed. I was so depressed, and my body just wouldn't function.

Jackie found that during her transition from being a teen to being a mother, her biggest challenge was being a single mother and raising two children on her own with no family support. Both of her daughters' fathers were incarcerated, and Jackie's father lived with her while he suffered from alcoholism and was recovering from a stroke. Jackie felt her transition was a personal challenge because she felt that everything fell on her. At times, she didn't feel she was capable of handling her responsibilities and duties, because of the ongoing stress.

> Um, even with all the depression and whatnot, I did feel like I was a strong person, because I had been through a lot even before I had children ... so I still felt like, you know, it was something I was going to be able to get through, but it was just at the time, you know, when I have them to support and not have the people to back me up.

Jackie had personal insight on what it was like to be homeless with her life being unstable and having numerous people she felt had betrayed her. She discussed her determination to not allow her emotions and feelings that she experienced during her transition to take her focus off her children. She had a burning desire to not let her children experience the life she had endured. Jackie constantly reminded herself of the life she had when she was growing up, and her determination to have a better life was a source of inner strength.

> Because, you know, I had already had a hard life myself, so I didn't want the same for my kids. I, um, I never, my whole life up until I had children, I never really was stable. I always went to my grandmother. That's when I swear I wasn't really stable, so, like, for me in my life, I added to like fifteen or twenty addresses.

Ironically, even with the instability she endured, Jackie was happy being a mother. The emotions and feelings she described during her transition to becoming a mother indicated that she felt good. She said she felt good because she was not going to walk out of her children's life like her mother had. She used the diminished relationship with her mother as the fuel to persevere through her challenges.

> I was happy, but when I came back to reality and said mess-up, I got bills to pay, I got a car to fix, I got food in the house, I got clothes I got to put on they back and my back … and that's when I would fall into, like, my depression stage.

Jackie felt good about being a mother and addressed her challenges as they were dealt to her. She tried reaching out to past mentors who assisted her through trying times. She said that she learned a lot about herself and that having her children not only changed her life but also made her a better person. She felt that because she grew up in the ghetto, she did not have to be the "ideal" teen mother or succumb to the negative ills often associated with and perceived by people who lived in subsidized housing. Jackie reflected on the images of teen mothers she encountered during her times of living in the ghetto and how those were the motivation for her not wanting to have that lifestyle for herself or her children.

Jackie was happy with the new changes she found in herself. She spoke about how important learning to be patient was to her (for example, not saying the first thing that came into her mind). She also recognized she was often angry and found herself being angry around her children. "Learning to let go of that in order to be happy with myself so I can be happy around my children and not be all mad all the time [is important]." Jackie took the time to learn how to "de-stress" herself so that she could make better choices in life. She admitted to having a quick temper and getting into physical altercations all the time. She now has a cognitive process to handle these situations.

> [I] think about why I was going through what I was going through. What I could do to change it, you know, how I needed to de-stress myself, relieving myself of all of that you know I could get where I was going to.

The Essence of Jackie's Experience

Jackie felt having her children was the best thing that had ever happened to her. She appeared to have found an inner peace with herself because of her desire to provide her children a stable life—one she had never experienced. Jackie said people who knew her spoke of how her attitude and personality changed for the better.

> Learning to let go of that in order to be happy with myself so I can be happy around my kids and not be all mad all the time. Having my kids were the best thing that happened to me. I don't cuss; I don't fight at all. I had a baby early, but it taught me a lot of positive things about myself.

Pam, Participant 8

Pam was a nineteen-year-old African American single mother with a ten-month old daughter. She became pregnant during her senior year in high school. Pam was able to graduate from high school and at the time the interview was conducted she was employed full time at a local fast food restaurant while living with a friend. Pam shared that her father asked her to leave the home when he found out she was pregnant. She said she had no support from her family and initially did not receive any support from her child's father. She did not have any type of relationship with her biological mother and was primarily raised by her father. Pam explained that during her pregnancy she moved three times, finally living with her aunt while she gave birth to her daughter; two months later she was living with a friend.

Pam said she did not experience any type of change in her life after having her child. Her life didn't change except that she gained weight. However, she did describe her challenges as stressful, which left her feeling nervous and scared. She shared that she was feeling stressed because of the lack of support she had and having a stressful full time job.

> Some of the stress was with my family. Some was my job. It was just mostly family and job. My dad, he wasn't … on the supportive side. He kicked me out the house. So I was basically living on the streets with my younger sister.

Pam described her transition from being a teen to becoming a mother as "easy." She professed she did not really experience any hardships during her transition. She said, "My transition was actually okay. It was … it was—it wasn't as easy, I mean wasn't as hard as some people made it out to be. It was kind of easy for me." Pam said she did not have support in taking care of her daughter, but she did not feel like her life changed since having her. She felt her transition into motherhood was easy. However, Pam spoke about the emotions and feelings she had during her transition, and she shared that she had many mixed emotions.

> I can say most of the time I was either sad and sometimes I just used to get angry for no reason. I just used to get angry at the fact that I didn't have a family that was supportive.

Pam also discussed often feeling angry because she felt she didn't have anyone in her corner. She said she was angry no one would listen to her, and people would just ignore her.

> As a support, just being there for me when I was emotional and angry. Nobody would get mad. Everybody'll understand where I was coming from. Just listen to me and hear what I got to say and think.

Pam described feeling isolated and alone after having her daughter, and the lack of support caused her to feel angry. When she felt like that, she felt alone: "But then sometimes I just be like, *It's my own world, and I am in it by myself.* I don't know (pause) just don't think about it (pause) I guess."

Pam did have a positive experience from having her baby. She recognized she had to make changes in her life. She realized that her first positive experience was coming to terms with having had her daughter and no longer getting angry over others' decisions. In reference to her change, she said, "I learned to stop getting mad. To learn to live with it and I made the choice. So, uh, I had to deal with it." She also attributed another positive change to becoming a mother—not going out and partying anymore. She realized that she had to make better decisions for herself and her child. Pam felt the change in thinking was positive for her.

I couldn't go out and live the party life anymore. I had big-girl responsibilities. Working, taking care of my child, couldn't spend my money on little stupid stuff anymore. I had to save my money!

The Essence of Pam's Experience

Pam said she became stronger when she became a mother, and it made her feel good about herself. She said others recognized she had become more responsible; she felt she matured a lot and enjoyed the compliments she received, because they boosted her self-esteem. Pam said her self-esteem also became bolstered while she was pregnant, because students at her school would tell her she was so pretty, and it made her feel good about herself. Overall, Pam reported that she was happy, and she was happy she could make her child happy. She admitted that when she first held her daughter she was in shock and could not believe she was a mother.

> After I had her and I was holding her tiny body in my hands, I was just like, *Wow. I can't believe you're my child.* I still do that to this day. I just look, and I be like, you're really mine.

Having her daughter gave Pam a sense of accomplishment. She summed this up when she said, "It's just to see … I just like the feeling of being able to see myself make my child happy."

Celena, Participant 9

Celena was an eighteen-year-old African American single mother with a one-year-old daughter. She became pregnant when she was sixteen and a sophomore in high school. At the time of the interview, Celena was in enrolled in a GED program at a local adult education center. She had recently found a job with a local fast food restaurant but was unhappy with it because of the low number of scheduled hours she was given. Celena complained that her child's father was not as supportive as she would have liked. Her mother assisted periodically with diapers and clothing, but Celena was the primary provider for her daughter. Celena expressed that she was happy she had her daughter but wished she had waited until she was better suited to take care of her.

She said that having her daughter changed her life drastically. One change she reported was that she gained confidence and became bolder. She gained her own voice by speaking up for herself when she gave birth.

> Well, I think 'cause I think it made me more like a little bit more bolder. Because before, I was, you know—you know I was a little shy, and ... well, I was a lot, I was a lot shy before. And you know, I let people walk, you know, over me and, you know, say whatever they wanted to say about me and stuff like that. And now, you know, now I just, you know, I don't let them do it as much. I have, you know, I have a voice now!

Celena said that she was still a teenager, and she still had to come to grips with being an adult as well. She realized she had to begin making adult-like decisions and behave differently from the teenager she was. She said, "I think I'm still a teenager. But, I have to make adult decisions. So I mean it was, you know it was ... it's kind of mixed. Like, like about, like about, sacrificing things for her."

Celena's transition to motherhood consisted of recognizing behavior she needed to change to parent her daughter. She realized she was still a teen and had teenage urges; however, in transforming into a responsible adult and parent, she knew she had to put her personal desires aside to benefit her daughter.

> Um, like if I want to, like, go to a party or something like that. Where I wouldn't go, like if she was sick or

something. Then I would have to stay with her, and you know I wouldn't leave her with somebody else or something like that. You know I would have to make a sacrifice, you know, to stay with her and wouldn't go out. Be an adult.

When asked if she considered herself a teen or an adult, Celena replied, "A teenager, 'cause I'm still, you know—I mean of course the age. But I'm still, you know, I still got the mind of a teenager. I'm still learning, but I'm still got to grow up." During her transitional phase, Celena shared that she was constantly worrying something bad was going to happen to her daughter. She kept thinking her daughter was going to die. She said, "So like, um, I don't know why. I was always thinking like, like she was going to die or something like that!" Celena said she felt stressed with dealing with her child's father, his lack of support, and the manner in which he handled matters. She felt he was very selfish and childish, and she ended their relationship. Celena mentioned that doing this gave her high levels of anxiety and that it was very stressful for her. She also mentioned being stressed about completing school and finding employment.

A major challenge for Celena during her transition was stress. She said she took her stress out on her daughter by raising her voice when she was upset. During the interview, she explained in full detail what she meant by *taking her anger out on her daughter*, which she explained meant using a harsh tone with her daughter. Celena gave examples of her tone with her daughter, and the researcher determined that this level of anger wouldn't harm her daughter. Celena explained it further:

Let's see, of course stress; let's see, of course I was sad. Sometimes I was mad. You know, sometimes I was of course sometimes, you know, take my anger out on her. I would, you know, yell at her.

Celena said her emotions would come all at once, and she did not have any way to deal with them. She did not have anyone to talk to about her problems except her sister. Her sister was her confidant for sounding off on all of the emotions and feelings she was enduring.

Celena explained another challenge she faced was parenting. She revealed she did not know what to do. She had no clue how to parent. When asked what challenges she experienced, she replied, "Just some more parenting. Umm, I didn't know what to do? I was like … I am a teenager, a kid … what am I supposed to do?" She stated she had an in-home counselor who taught her about parenting and taking care of her baby. She said she also learned how to not put other people before her daughter. She recognized it was no longer about her needs, but the needs of her daughter. She said the biggest hurdle she overcame was feeling that she needed her daughter's father to help her for her daughter to survive. She said once she got over that notion, she was able to move forward. She also said she was still in shock that she has a daughter and that she still has not grasped the fact she is actually someone's mother.

Her reaction to being a proud mother was, "Well, I—I don't know 'cause like it's like to this day it's still like *wow*."

The Essence of Celena's Experience

Even though she was biologically a mother, Celena still viewed herself as a teenager. She still had her teenage thoughts and desires; however, she found inner strength to resist some of the desires and to instead parent her child. Having a baby gave Celena confidence and self-esteem she had never had. Through the birth of her child, Celena recognized new thoughts and feelings she had not experienced before becoming a mother.

Lisa, Participant 10

Lisa was an eighteen-year-old African American single mother with a three-year-old daughter. She became pregnant with her first child when she was fifteen years old and a freshman in high school. She was in the process of completing high school at the time of the interview. She also had a part-time job at a daycare center and was proud she was able to provide for her daughter. Lisa's biological mother and father assisted her with supporting her daughter.

Lisa's daughter's father and his family were supportive of Lisa during and after her pregnancy. Overall, she had significant support with her daughter. She endured personal changes during her transition from being a teen to becoming a mother, including episodes of personal enlightenment. This participant felt ashamed of being pregnant and did not want to go to school, because she was the only pregnant student there at the time. Ironically, she was forced to attend school by the truancy department, and she ended up being a confidante for the students at her school. Lisa felt proud since she was in the position to help other girls going through similar situations at her school.

> So to me it was, kind of, a, you know, big deal, but at the same time they was kind of helpful for me because I came to accept the fact that I was having a child because since everyone else was, like, coming to me and asking for help. So I took it to the point that I [was] blessed to get pregnant.

Lisa had an epiphany and realized that her being pregnant was not as bad as she thought. She said, "Being a teenager then, I feel to me that getting pregnant came at the right time." Lisa did, however, recognize she had to change her ways because she was a mother. However, it was hard and took awhile for her to recognize that she was responsible for another life and had to make better decisions for herself and her child.

> My social life outside of school was terrible; I was always getting into fights. So to me it felt like it was a blessing and came at the right, exact, same time,

> a good time to change me because when she came,
> it took me to think twice about doing crazy things.
> At the same token, every decision that I made was
> for her.

Lisa began to embrace her role as a mother—not only with making better choices for herself but also recognizing the fact that she had dual roles to uphold: teen and mother. Describing her attire, she said, "So the tight clothes, the booty shorts I will, you know, I still wear but I know I need to show that I'm still a mother." Lisa's interview resonated with the themes of her recognition that she was transforming into another person with additional responsibilities. She appreciated that having her child was a positive aspect in her life that helped her develop into a better person. She described the experience by saying, "So I'm kind of glad that I actually did go through with my pregnancy, because it's not, I don't know, where I could have been right now."

Lisa received assistance and support from her mother and relied on her mother's triumphant strength as a single mother to be the best mother she could be. She said, "My feelings in being a mother I get to go through what my mom went through with me, but I also get to change, break the chain." Lisa recognized the hardships her mother had endured as a single parent and tried not to make the same mistakes. She used her mother as a symbol of strength and power; however, she wanted to break the cycle of unsuccessful single motherhood that loomed in her family and neighborhood.

> Me being a teen mother now—well, being a parent,
> anyway—is a little difficult, being a mother, but I feel
> what my mom went through, but at the same token, I
> don't mind, because the simple fact is I'm not missing
> out on anything. I'm basically here to see everything
> from born to when she turns eighteen.

Lisa used her daughter as a positive motivator and appeared to fully understand that there was a clear distinction between her being a teenager and her being a teen mother. She embraced the hardships and difficult moments and made them positive teachable moments for herself.

> The idea of having bad times, experience being a teen mom, and that I have messed up some, but I do not regret because it made me [much harder]. It made me realize the fact she [her daughter] sees everything I do.

Lisa discussed numerous positive thoughts and concepts when describing her transition to motherhood compared with the other participants. She had support, and she made positive situations out of her negative encounters—not losing focus on the fact she was now a mother. Lisa summed up her transition best when she said,

> So that's when I realized I was a mother. That's when I realized, for a while, I got somebody I've got to take care of; I've got to support them. And so me being a teen mother, I was going to be able to be no more wild fighting and I would have to cut down on the partyin' or hangin' with friends; I have to more, focus on—now I got somebody, I have to can raise and show what to do and what not to do. So I'm kind of, like, happy to be a teen mother to the fact that it changed my life from the age fifteen up!

The Essence of Lisa's Experience

Lisa felt her daughter came at the right time in her life. She also realized that in her neighborhood and with her own mother, single motherhood did not always end on a positive chord; however, Lisa used the negative stigma as a point of reference and perseverance. She was determined to use her pregnancy for positivity, motivation, and for the common good of her peers. Lisa embraced her role as mother in the way she thought, how she handled situations, and even how she dressed. She wanted to set a good example for her daughter.

Nina, Participant 11

Nina was a nineteen-year-old African American single mother with a fourteen-month-old son. She became pregnant when she was sixteen years old and was a senior in high school when she gave birth to her son. She was originally from New York. After getting out of foster care, she came to live with her mother in Richmond. She was in the process of attempting to graduate from high school and looking for a job. Nina lived with her mother and four siblings. She was also trying to obtain her own apartment. Nina said that some of her family assisted her when she had her son, but she also received help from the family of the child's father. Nina described her initial change as her bettering herself. She admitted at first she was a tomboy before having a baby. While she was pregnant, she was complimented on her beauty and that made her feel good about herself, so she became "more girly." She said, "I would say *better myself*, because beforehand, I was a tomboy. I really didn't care about certain stuff." However, Nina did mention that being pregnant made her feel beautiful, and she liked the attention she was getting.

Nina described the challenges she faced as frustrating. She experienced severe mood swings, and she felt lost at times because she didn't know how she was feeling. She said, "At first I was, um, in denial. Then I was happy, then I was frustrated … then I was sad, then I was happy again." Nina said that during her transition from teen to teen mother she felt angry quite frequently. She shared that she was often angry at individuals for the comments they made about her. Then she learned to listen and accept help from those who were actually trying to help and she learned to ignore those who made negative comments about her. She recognized there were other pressing issues she had to address.

> I went into Mommy mode, I guess you could say. You
> stop worrying about what, like, other people think,
> and like not getting so defensive and angry toward
> people, because, like, realizing you need the help, so
> it's not going to get you nowhere to get angry and
> defensive all the time.

Nina recognized after having her baby that her personal life had changed. One issue left her feeling sad was the loss of her social life and her old friends. She said her friends were around her while she was pregnant, but they no longer came to visit her after she had her baby. She described the situation with this response:

> Where's all my friends? Everybody who was in my
> face when I was pregnant, but now when I need them
> to help me, they're not here! Then when the baby's
> born, like, they don't want to be around my house.

Nina had a rocky relationship with her child's father but received a great deal of support from his family. She said her family did the best they could to assist her as well, but she still dealt with feelings of sadness. She was sad about her new situation, new role, and new responsibilities.

> But there was, like, sadness because it was like there
> were times when I wanted to go places and couldn't
> just drive him up and go. But there were times when
> I could do that, but there's like when you can't do it
> all the time, you know, it gets boring; like, I'm bored.

Nina felt she had grown as a person in a positive direction since becoming a mother. She recognized that there was room for her own personal growth, and she knew certain characteristics had to change. Nina also recognized she had to begin to put her child first and make decisions that would positively affect them both. She said, "Sometimes you just got to take certain stuff, and, you know, certain stuff that you probably wouldn't take before having the baby. So basically just thinking about my child first, and you know, let everything else work out." Nina explained that she became more independent and learned to be more patient toward others, and these characteristics were positive and beneficial to her.

> I had to teach myself more independence ... me being ... first, first I had, I had to teach, and I'm still teaching myself; I calmed down a lot. I'm getting a little bit better; I can be way more better, is with patience. Because I get aggravated too fast. Because I'm always yelling at whatever doesn't go my way.

The Essence of Nina's Experience

Nina felt proud when she gave birth to her son and felt good about herself. Not only did she develop cognitively into a mother, but also her style of dress and outlook on life changed once she became pregnant and gave birth to her son. Nina summed up her experience of being a mother when she said, "Every time I watch him as he grew, I'm like, wow, that's my son. It made me feel good."

Bev, Participant 12

Bev was a twenty-year-old African American single mother with a thirty-five-month-old daughter. She was pregnant with her daughter while she was a junior in high school. Bev was a high school graduate who at the time of the interview was unemployed but attending vocational school. She was very outspoken about the lack of support she received from her family and her child's father when she had her daughter.

However, Bev was placed in the custody of the local Department of Social Services foster care because of her own mother's neglect, and she remained in a foster home during her pregnancy and after the birth of her child. She received support from her social worker and foster mother. Bev still felt overwhelmed during her transition into motherhood. Bev described her experience as follows: "I was still in high school, so I had focus on making sure my grades were right and homework, and at the same time this baby's always crying. It was just too much." She appeared to agonize over the fact she had to share herself with someone else. She summed up her experience. "My biggest challenge was coming out of my *me* thing." Bev explained her challenges of being a teen mother as frustrating. She struggled with grasping the concept that she had to be responsible and care for another human being. She became upset about putting herself in a giving position because she admitted she was selfish.

> I think it got more so frustrating and overwhelming. Because, like, at first it was just like me-me-me, me-me-me, and either my way or the highway, and I'm selfish—I'll be the first one to admit it; I'm very selfish. But, like, after you have a baby it's, I'll go, "Oh, the baby needs this, the baby needs to be fed, the baby needs to be wiped," so it's like an adjustment period. It's something that has to grow on you.

Bev's challenge of motherhood was realizing the numerous parental responsibilities and the level of need a child requires. She quickly had to learn the difference between her needs and her wants. "And learning the difference between a need and a want. Yes. Because, like, I wanted to do this and I wanted to do that." Bev described her transition from being a teen to becoming a mother as "god-awful." She confessed she did not like kids. "It was god-awful! I don't like kids. No. Seriously. But I do not like kids. I try to deal with them, but I don't." When Bev described the challenges, she became visibly animated and adamant about how much of an effect early childbearing could have on teenage life.

Bev put the concept of her being a teen mother into perspective. "So it's just like me losing who I am and having to change into the one thing that I dislike the most was, it was hard. Like, it was awful. That's the only word I can use!" she said. Bev struggled with who she had to become. She was not happy with her transformation, and living in a foster home was overwhelming to her. She spoke about losing herself and not knowing who or what she was.

> My totally different person is, this is an awful word to use, and excuse my language, but I was a bitch about it. Like, I just did not want to lose. Like, I still wanted to be me; I still wanted to have, like, I still wanted to be me. I still wanted to have fun and be carefree. But after about, it's like that tug and pull and struggle; you just give it up. Because it's no use. You're fighting a losing battle, and your life not being fun and or carefree. But after about, it's like that tug and pull and struggle; you just give it up!

Bev described the emotions and feelings about her transition as "frustration, frustration, frustration." She appeared to feel trapped in her new role of motherhood. She spoke about missing her teen life that was now being overshadowed by maternal duties. She said, "Since I wanted to be high (use marijuana) even though I was pregnant and not pay attention to the parts in classes, not pay attention to the mothering books. A child crying irks my last nerves." Bev described the sound of a crying child as "like nails on a chalkboard to me." She struggled with embracing her role as a mother and during the interview shared that she still did not fully feel like a mother. She struggled with establishing a bond with her daughter. Bev spoke of the lack of a bond she had with her own mother because of her mother's drug use. She struggled with knowing exactly what to do as a mother besides taking care of basic needs.

> And for a long time I did not have that bond with my baby. I had to make it there, like, I had to force it

[laughing]. Because I just did not care to be a mom!
Like, she's older, and truth be told, I still don't care
to be a mom.

Bev did find something positive in the process of her child being born. She said she was no longer being reckless; instead, she was focusing on her daughter and thinking about the consequences of her actions. Bev stated she would get into physical altercations at the sound of any wrong word, but now she said she thinks more "logically." She thinks about getting arrested or her daughter being placed in custody with social services. "If I catch a charge, where my baby going to be while I'm around out doing community service? Or if I go to CPS [Child Protective Services], that's going to be money being taken away from her." Not only did Bev's thinking change, but also her behavior and attitude changed for the better. She described herself as being a very loud, uncaring, ruthless female with the slang title of being "Ratchet." Bev described this transformation as follows:

> I think my attitude's a lot better. I know my attitude
> was ratcheted. Because at first it's just, I just like real
> ratcheted and I ain't care. Like now, I think, I'm
> humbler now; I'm not a humble person at all!

Bev began to focus more on her life. She graduated from high school third in her class, and she also received two scholarship offers for college, which she disclosed after the interview. Bev was the first person in her biological family to graduate from high school.

> I had no intentions on going to college, like, I got
> into ... more and more into school. I was like, whoa,
> college?

Maybe, what's up. But in the same sense, it stopped me because I couldn't go away. It's only a select few schools that accept parents with their child, and I just—I don't have nobody to leave her with, nor do I trust anybody to leave her with. So I graduated from high school, the first in my family, and took class at community college ... work ... you know, the boring stuff adults supposed to do!

The Essence of Bev's Experience

Bev became more focused on her daughter and less focused on herself. "I focused more on doing what I needed to do to better us, instead of doing what pleases me." Bev appeared to find solace in her ongoing and developing role of motherhood. She recognized what was required of her as a mother, but—unlike the other participants—Bev decided to hang on to her teenage role longer.

Composite Structural Descriptions

The composite structural description provides an understanding of the essence of all the participants' experiences and the phenomenon as described in the individual structural descriptions. The composite descriptions that follow describe how the participants as a group viewed developing a maternal identity and their transitional process from being a teen to becoming a mother. The themes and corresponding meaning units provide the overall summary of the data analysis.

Composite Structural Descriptions for Research Question #1

The composite structural description that follows addresses research question #1, which questions how adolescent mothers develop their maternal-role identity. The composite structural description describes the experiences of the twelve participants as they developed their maternal identity. The themes and corresponding meaning units provide the overall summary of the data analysis.

Analysis of the data revealed three composite nomothetic themes that emerged from the twelve participants' descriptions of their transitions to motherhood. Research question #1 is: "How do adolescent mothers develop maternal-role identity?" The nomothetic that emerged regarding this question consisted of (a) experiencing conflicting identities, (b) defining a new and positive sense of self, and (c) accepting maternal role duties and responsibilities.

The nomothetic themes, along with the ideographic theme and natural meaning units, are presented in narrative form and in table 2. The themes are supported with statements made by the participants to provide a clear description of the phenomenon as it was experienced during the participant's transition.

Table 2 – Research Question #1, Nomothetic Themes

Nomothetic Themes	Natural Meaning Units	Frequency
Experiencing conflicting identities	I know as a mother, as a teen mother, that even though it's hard and you want to still be that teen, it's, basically it's helping you to show you that life is really no joke and that life is really here and that it's, kind of, hard. (Participant 10)	10 of 12
Defining a new and positive sense of self	I guess I find myself, like I said, more mature, more confident. (Participant 6) Having my baby gave me a voice. (Participant 5)	12 of 12
Accepting maternal role duties and responsibilities	I had to bite the bullet and stop doing all the wild stuff I was doing, partying, hanging out late, doing whatever whenever, drinking, smoking, going out to chill with friends, all that had to stop! I was like nawwhh, I want my life back. (Participant 3)	11 of 12

Note: Nomothetic themes = frequently reoccurring themes stated by participants; natural meaning units = words or statement specified by each individual participant; frequency = the number of participants who shared the same responses.

Theme 1

Experiencing conflicting identities was a nomothetic theme with all twelve participants. The participants spoke about their struggles of toggling between their desires to "still be a teen," to continue to hang out with friends and party, and to act on their own free will. These were the responses that came up with participants when they described their new duties and responsibilities as mothers. All twelve of the participants mentioned the effects their babies had on their lives. Four of the participants candidly stated how they wanted their lives back or how they still wanted to be a teen. Participant 9 stated she still felt like a teenager, whereas participant 12 spoke about not feeling like a mother yet. The participants' responses reflected the mixed feelings of whom they were and what role they were supposed to play. Teenagers are often egocentric and are impulsive with their decision-making; they have personal scripts they have to adhere to. However, motherhood has identified scripts, roles, and responsibilities. Many of the participants struggled with understanding and grasping the concepts and scripted roles of being a mother.

Theme 2

Defining a new and positive self was a nomothetic theme that resonated with changes in cognition, behavior, and views of life. All of the twelve participants identified positive changes in themselves that they attributed to having a child. Participant 10 felt her concepts of mothering were going to break a cycle that she had in her family and that other mothers had in her neighborhood. Five of the twelve participants grew up without their biological mothers, and they were determined to be there for their children because of feeling the brunt of not having their mothers around as they grew up. Learning to think before acting was a positive attribute for nine of the twelve participants. Four of them said they used to become physically violent with others when things did not go the way they planned; however, since having their babies, they learned to think about the consequences of becoming violent and being placed in dangerous situations. Participant twelve explained this process of thinking before acting.

> I can't just, for now, but I can't spill out emotions now. Now I got to be more logical because at the end of the day, it's this person that I got to think about. Like, if I go to jail, who be there for my baby? If I catch a charge, where my baby going to be while I'm around out doing community service or if I got to PSS, that's going to be money being taken away from her.

Participants 5 and 9 spoke of how having their babies gave them confidence and a voice they never had before becoming a mother. Participant 5 explained, "Yes, most definitely, after … having her I changed … got a voice. I'm more confident in myself." Ten of the twelve participants shared that learning patience was an important and positive change in their behavior. They spoke about not having had patience before having children but developing it as a result of being mothers.

Seven of the participants started thinking about and planning their future since becoming mothers.

Theme 3

Accepting a maternal role and developing maternal responsibilities was a theme that resonated throughout all of the interview questions. Each participant recognized at least at one point during her transition she was now "a mother." Either through decision making, behavior, or actions, they all encountered moments in which they realized they were now mothers. They realized they had someone else depending on them now, and they couldn't afford to make decisions that might be detrimental to them.

Participant 2 said, "I guess that fact that it's not about me anymore. When I made decisions based on my son's needs and not mine, that's when it realized to me I was mom." Many of the participants spoke about particular events that took place in their lives that "woke them up" and made them realize they were mothers. Some of the situations were life-threatening. Participant 1 realized this after being at a party where something occurred—she could have died—and she thought about who would raise her child if something happened to her. Recalling the situation, articipant 1 said, "There was an incident that happened at one party, and I was like, *I could've died*. I wouldn't be here. And then I thought of my daughter. If I would've died, who would've took care of her?"

> Participants 3, 5, 6, 7, 10, and 12 all spoke about using drugs and engaging in physical altercations. They spoke of how they had to avoid that type of behavior because they had children, so someone else now depended on them.

Participant 5 discussed her rationale to stop using drugs because of her daughter:

> I'm not doing drugs now, like I was before. Oh, yes. Oh, yes. You know, I used to think that there was nothing out here for me—you know, that I was going to be nobody, but now, you know, seeing her, looking at her every day, you know, you're doing something for a reason. A whole lot of inspiration, a whole lot of it.

Participant 10 also spoke about having to go into surgery and recognizing she had another person to consider other than herself; she realized she had to make changes in her life. Participant 4 explained how being a mother made her more responsible; before having her child, she was considered to be very irresponsible. Eleven of the participants accepted their newfound roles as mothers at varying times during their transitions. Eight of the mothers experienced it through empathy when they first held their baby in their arms. Two of the mothers had traumatic events, such as being in a party that was riddled with gunshots—and the other before having emergency surgery. One participant knew she was a mother, but she felt like she was still a teen and thought like a teen. One participant was still coping with the fact that she was a mother. Six of the twelve participants did not grow up with their biological mothers, and one participant's mother had passed away when she was younger. Five of them had been in foster care. Three participants discussed their motivation to be a good mother because of feeling abandoned by their natural mothers and wanting to thwart the same type of childhood imposed on them by their own mothers.

Composite Structural Descriptions
for Research Question #2

The composite structural description that follows addresses research question #2, which questions how adolescent mothers describe the experience of transitioning from being a teen to being a teen mother. Analysis of the data revealed three composite nomothetic themes emerging from twelve participants' descriptions of their transitional experiences (Table 3). Research question #2 asked, "How do adolescent mothers describe the experience of transitioning from being a teen to becoming a teen mother?" The nomothetic that emerged consisted of (a) experiencing conflicting identities, (b) defining a new and positive sense of self, (c) accepting maternal role duties and responsibilities.

Table 3 – Research Question #2, Nomothetic Themes

Nomothetic Themes	Natural Meaning Units	Frequency
Constantly needing support	Because maybe I wouldn't have went through all the things that I went through I had a better support system that was a big problem for me and my baby. (Participant 6)	11 of 12
Experiencing emotional cycling	Um, I can say most of the time I was either sad and sometimes I just used to get angry for no reason. (Participant 8)	11 of 12
Experiencing mental health symptomology	Sometimes I won't want to get out of bed. I was so depressed and my body just wouldn't function right. (Participant 7)	11 of 12

Theme 4

Constantly needing support was a nomothetic theme that resonated with all twelve participants. Three levels of support were identified by participants: support from their own parents, support from their child's father, and support from other family members or mentors. Additional types of support emerged from the data to include various types of support needed or received.

Four of the twelve participants mentioned they had support from either their biological mother or father.

Two participants mentioned receiving help from their biological fathers. The family support ranged from biological parents to siblings, grandparents, and aunts. Three of the participants said they received support from other relatives, such as their aunts or sisters.

Family support appeared to be a significant factor for the participants during their transition. Family involvement was significant in that it provided them financial support, resources, and emotional support. The emotional support had two effects on the participants—either positive or negative. The positive elements were that the participants were recognized as a source of inspiration, which helped elevate their self-concepts and senses of self-esteem. However, sometimes negative factors accompanied the support and affected the participants, who were filled with shame, guilt, and embarrassment. Family members verbalized their feelings about the participants having their children and being unprepared and not responsible to handle parenting duties.

Having support from their children's father was a key element that all participants discussed. It appeared to be an important factor—not only in terms of financial support but also with regard to the mother having a companion or the father being there for their child. The lack of the child's father's presence for nine of the twelve participants was also the root of stress, anger, and betrayal. Participants 3, 4, and 12 especially focused on their children's fathers not being present and how this affected them emotionally. They did not create their child alone, and they were puzzled as to why they would have to raise the baby alone.

The support included assistance with their child, bringing supplies such as diapers, and babysitting. Nine of the twelve participants did not receive any support from their children's fathers at all, while three of them did. Of the three participants who received support, one of the children's fathers lived with her, and the other two received assistance from the father's family.

Finally, the adolescent mothers' need for emotional support also emerged from the data—and their need for companionship and social peer interaction. Companionship and social peer interaction went away for five of the participants when they had their babies, which caused feelings of abandonment and loneliness. The lack of stable housing was an issue for five of the twelve participants. At least one participant said she did not have stable housing during her transition and had to live in multiple homes.

Theme 5

Experiencing a cycling of emotions was a theme that resonated with all of the participants (table 4). All twelve participants said that during their transition they felt uncertain, unsure, lost, and nervous at one time or another. Many of the responses focused on their situations dealing with parenting their children, providing the basic needs for their children (food, housing, and clothing), and changing their self-perceptions. Eleven of the twelve participants experienced anxiety and frustration. The one participant who did not mention feeling anxiety and frustration was participant 4, who mentioned having full support and help from her mother and father. In addition to experiencing anxiety and frustration, ten participants expressed feeling stressed from the transition. The two participants who did not mention their transition as being stressful were participants 4 and 10.

Many of the participants experienced cycles of emotions in which they felt sad, happy, sad, angry, and then sad again. Eleven of them referenced experiencing this emotional cycling at various times during their transition. Surprisingly, many of the participants were able to calm themselves down when they were cycling anger or sadness if they thought of their children or looked at them. This made them smile, feel happy, or made them feel good about themselves. Participant 7 recognized that holding grudges against people who hurt her kept her angry often. She described making herself happy as follows: "Learning to let go of that [holding grudges against others] to be happy with myself, so I can be happy around my kids and not be all mad all the time." Participant 3 provided a more vivid account of this process when she shared the following:

> It was hard to find good motivation. It was hard. I just didn't like anybody, and people stop being around me because I always had an attitude. My baby made me mad ... but he made me smile ... seeing his face and him spitting for no reason made me laugh all the time.

Table 4 – Experiencing Emotional Cycling

Participant No.	Natural Meaning Units
2	I would just go, you know, angry, sad, happy.
5	I went through many emotions, angry, sad, happy, depressed, you know, postpartum thing hit me, too, so I mean . . .,"
6	I had a lot of different emotions. Some was happy, sometimes I was happy. Sometime I was sad.
8	Um, I can say most of the time I was either sad and sometimes I just used to get angry for no reason;
9	Um, let's see, of course I was sad. Sometimes I was mad."
11	Then, I was happy, then I was frustrated Then I was sad, then I was happy again.

Theme 6

Many of the adolescent mothers experienced mental health symptoms during their transition to motherhood. Four of the participants were diagnosed with a mental health condition; two were diagnosed bipolar, and two were diagnosed with postpartum depression (for which they sought treatment from a therapist). When describing their emotions and feelings during their transition, the participants spoke of hopelessness, ongoing worrying, feeling overwhelmed, mood swings, and a lack of confidence in their parenting. All of these are common symptoms new mothers suffer from when experiencing postpartum depression. For example, participant 3 spoke about having good, bad, and down days. "My down days, like, depending on how it was, like, if I woke up in bad mood, I was a bad mood the entire day."

Participant 5 experienced depression from the stress of being a mother. She realized the emotional task of mothering was too overwhelming for her, and she sought treatment from a therapist. She said,

The depression is because it was something new to me. Being a mom, it was sad, mostly, you know, because I was sad, confused. This is something new, and you have to learn to deal with it and know when it is coming on. I went to therapy and got some pills.

Participant 1 shared her experience of dealing with the emotional task of motherhood while balancing Bipolar I disorder. She gave a vivid account of what it was like dealing with her disorder.

Um, I suffer from bipolar, so it was like I had this state of mind where I would be like, *I don't want this thing*, like one part of the time, and then the second part of the time, I'd be like, *I do*. It was like I was just looking back and forth …

Because every day, I deal with my own mood swings. And I know that's not good, and sometimes I find myself ready to snap, and I have to remember I can't, because you know I have to think about my kids and how they feel with me going off. So I don't want to go off ' round them. I send them away so they won't think, *Momma going crazy*.

Summary

This phenomenological study explored the experiences of urban adolescent mothers as they transitioned into motherhood. The chapter provided the results of the data gathering and analysis, which yielded the results of the phenomenon that occurred within this population. Six nomothetic themes emerged from the participants' natural meaning units and the ideographic themes that provided the overall essences of what urban adolescent mothers encountered and endured as they transitioned from being a teen, transformed into a mother, and developed a maternal-role identity. The six themes were

(a) experiencing conflicting identities, (b) defining a new and positive sense of self, (c) accepting maternal role duties and responsibilities, (d) constantly needing support, (e) experiencing emotional cycling, and (f) experiencing mental health symptomology.

Face-to-face semistructured interviews were conducted with the adolescent mothers to capture the essences of their experiences. The information gathered in the interviews was transcribed and reviewed by the participants to ensure accuracy and validity. The transcripts where coded using an adaptation of the procedures for data analysis for phenomenological study described by Giorgi (1985, 2009), Moustakas (1994), and Stones (1979). The data were organized, analyzed, and synthesized to yield the results of the natural meaning units, which were then used to analyze and identify the ideographic themes. Finally, themes were analyzed to yield the six nomothetic themes relayed in this study.

The information in this chapter was presented in the form of narrative descriptions and tables as they related to the two research questions: "How do teen mothers develop maternal-role identity?" and "How do teen mothers describe the experience of transitioning from being a teen to becoming a teen mother?" The individual structural descriptions provided the participants' individual accounts of their thoughts, perceptions, and feelings about their transition to motherhood. A composite structural description summarized the phenomenon experienced by the group as a whole. The next and final chapter will provide a summary of the research along with recommendations and implications for future research.

Chapter 5

SUMMARY, CONCLUSIONS, AND RECOMMENDATIONS

Introduction

This phenomenological study identified the experiences of urban adolescent mothers regarding their transitional process of becoming a mother and developing a maternal identity. The researcher used the following two questions to guide this study: How do teen mothers develop maternal-role identity? How do teen mothers describe the experience of transitioning from being a teen to being a teen mother? This chapter discusses the results of the data collected as they correlate to the theoretical frameworks used for this study. This chapter also includes a summary of the findings, the limitations of the study, a discussion of the findings as they correlate with the current literature, implications for future practice, recommendations for assisting adolescent mothers, recommendations for future research, and the conclusion.

Limitations of the Study

Because this study was qualitative, it had several limitations. The sample population used for this study was very restrictive. The study lacks generalizability and transferability because of the purposeful sampling, small sample size, and subjective data collection processes. The sample consisted of twelve urban adolescent mothers ages eighteen to twenty-two, of whom ten were African American. The study documented the experiences of these urban African American mothers, as well as one Caucasian and one Native American/Pacific Islander mother.

Given the specific sampling pool and qualitative inquiry used by the researcher, this study is limited because of the restrictive nature of the sample population used. The results of this study could not be used to address a general population, because it only provides insight into the experiences of twelve urban adolescent mothers who lack ethnic diversity.

Additional factors that impose on the generalizability of the study include socioeconomic class status, because the adolescent mothers from this study were identified as being from a lower socioeconomic class status. Furthermore, the demographic area included participants only from the urban portion of a central location within the state. The study does not explore adolescent fathers' perceptions; nor does it offer quantitative or statistical information about the phenomenon investigated.

Although the findings from this study focus only on a specific population of adolescent mothers, they do replicate with previous studies conducted on adolescent mothers (Aiello and Lancaster 2007; Hallman 2007; Kennedy 2006; Lesser et al. 2003; Noria et al. 2007; Sadler and Cowlin 2003; Shanok and Miller 2007a; Taylor 2010). The findings from this study provide insight into the transitional process of adolescent mothers and the process of developing maternal-role identity for those working with adolescent mothers—specifically the researcher who works in a residential setting and provides community outreach services to urban adolescent mothers.

Results and Discussion of the Findings

Summary of the Findings

The goal of this study was to investigate the experiences of urban adolescent mothers as they transitioned into motherhood and developed their maternal identities. The participants were twelve urban adolescent mothers aged eighteen to twenty-two. Racial/ethnic backgrounds were as follows: one Caucasian, one Native American/Pacific Islander, and ten African American women. Data analysis uncovered reoccurring phenomenal experiences shared by a majority of the participants: accepting maternal roles and duties, emotional cycling, and varying levels support. These themes were identified to have direct and indirect effects on the teen mothers' transitional processes as they grew to accept their new identities. Six reoccurring themes emerged from the individual and composite structural descriptions: (a) experiencing conflicting identities, (b) defining a new and positive sense of self, (c) accepting maternal role duties and responsibilities, (d) constantly needing support, (e) experiencing emotional cycling, and (f) experiencing mental health symptomology.

The findings from this study suggest that the transition to motherhood for adolescent mothers consists of cognitive fluctuation (ruminating thoughts, feelings, and emotions about their new roles as mothers and contemplation of their roles as adolescents); behavioral transformation (making decisions and taking actions that were more positive and goal-oriented than in the past); and recognizing the continual need for consistency, stabilization, and support to assist them with the psychological paradox of their dueling worlds of being an adolescent and becoming a mother. The analysis of their experiences revealed that the role of being a mother involved the participants' not only making changes in their daily behaviors by force but also facing a transformation within themselves. The transformation involved cognitive and behavioral changes that enlightened and empowered them to be better young women overall. This personal transformation entailed the adolescent mothers' changing their entire outlooks on life, eliminating negative and high-risk behaviors (including drugs and violence), and making better decisions and choices in life that were beneficial to them and their children. Participant 7 provided her overview of a transformational and behavioral change:

> I just sort of like that, at the time, you know, with me being the way I was, you know, wanting to be round the street and wanting to hang out with drug dealers, gang bangers, and what not. I feel like it was at this point and time a way of God telling me this is not the life that I need to live, so you know, I wasn't running. You know, it was like everybody say, when opportunity knocks at the door, you got to answer it, and I just thought like it was the opportunity to me to get out of the lifestyle that I was living.

Varying types of support—whether emotional, financial, or social—were all themes that came up in the descriptions the adolescent mothers gave of their transformations and transitions. These three levels of support were pertinent in determining the outcome of their transitions to motherhood. In some cases, some of the participants who reported having emotional and financial support were found to have fewer reports of anxiety or stress, and they felt happy and appreciated becoming mothers. In other cases, participants without emotional or social support reported feeling a mixture of emotions: loneliness, depression, stress, and frustration. Therefore, support had a dramatic effect on the participants' transitions to motherhood. Support reported as "consistent" was the most effective for the new mothers, while support received sporadically made very little impact on the overall transition. For example, participant 4 constantly received emotional, financial, and social support from her family. She loved her experience of becoming a mother, and she had the full support of her mother and father. The majority of her shared experiences were happy in nature.

> And I ... like, school, and then having her, having to
> come home and take care of her and working. That
> was a lot too. But I mean, I had a lot of help, so I—I
> was never really stressed. My mom, my dad, and
> family, like, I have a really good family, so we were
> all there for me.

The same situation existed for participants 2 and 10. They had emotional and social support from their mothers and their children's fathers or fathers' family. This support helped them complete school, and they shared tales of happiness. In other cases, participants receiving inconsistent and sporadic support continually sought additional support, which caused emotional grief. Participant 8 provided an account of her challenges as an example of lacking emotional and social supports:

> Not having that supportive backbone from my family.
> Um, maybe having a job before I actually had the
> baby. Just having steady support. And not be all over
> the place. As a support, just being there for me when I
> was emotional and angry and nobody would get mad.
> Everybody'll understand where I was coming from.
> Just listen to me and hear what I got to say and think.

The adolescent mothers' accounts supported the existing literature that they experience many changes in their lives during early childbearing (Brehey and Stephens 2007; Cox et al. 2008). The results from this study expand on previous studies that revealed the positive outcomes that came from early childbearing (Edin and Kefalas 2005; Shanok and Miller 2007a; SmithBattle 2010; Wright and Davis 2006), as opposed to the negative perceptions and outcomes that have been concluded in research for the past two decades (Deutscher et al. 2006; Coley and Chase-Lansdale 1998; Corcoran and Kunz 1997; Furstenberg et al. 1987; Hanna 2001; Oxford et al. 2005). In addition, the urban adolescent mothers' candid responses revealed explicit situations that affected them in both positive and negative ways.

Even though the participants lacked support, struggled with graduating from high school, did not have stable housing, and experienced hardships in obtaining employment, they still managed to motivate themselves to persevere, remain positive, and make adult decisions. The participants' accounts of experiences revealed their resiliency and perseverance. They described in detail how others would frown on them, yet how they would look at their children and use them as a source of motivation to do the right things and make positive decisions to better themselves. All twelve of the participants shared stories in which they persevered and used their children as a source of inspiration to combat the ongoing problems they endured during their transition. Similar studies have found resilience in adolescent mothers (Black and Ford-Gilboe 2004; Borkowski 2007; Hess, Papas, and Black 2002), which in turn led to better outcome— not only for the adolescent mothers but also for their children.

Relationship of the Findings to the Literature

The findings from this study are consistent with and support findings from previous literature on early childbearing in adolescents (Clemmens 2002; Hurlburt and McDonald 1997; Kaye 2008; SmithBattle 2007). The results add to the pool of research about the transitional processes experienced by adolescent mothers (Barratt et al. 1996; Brubaker and Wright 2006; Hurlburt and McDonald 1997; Jacobs and Mollborn 2012; Larson 2004). In addition to adding credence to the transitional process of adolescent mothers, the results provide insight and address the issues of personal dynamics, emotional status, and cognitive processes adolescent mothers endure during their transformation to motherhood. (Hurlburt and McDonald 1997; Kaiser and Hayes 2004; Oxford et al. 2005; Sadler and Cowlin 2003). Rosendgard et al. (2006) suggested future qualitative studies explore more in-depth interviews to understand the complexities of the advantages and disadvantages of teen parenting. Noria et al.

(2007) reviewed one hundred studies of adolescent mothers and found they revealed developmental struggles—such as immature affective relationships and hostile interactions with peers and family—that had a "synergistic effect" on the maternal development and led to problematic maternal adjustment (p. 44). They suggested further research to understand the dynamics of adolescent mothers' development.

Finally, Logsdon et al. (2008) found that adolescent mothers felt their new roles as parents often brought a great deal of stress and socio-emotional maladjustment. They suggested that additional research should investigate the variables associated with treatment of depressive symptoms in postpartum adolescent mothers. Overall, the results of the study provide an additional stepping-stone to the research in understanding more in depth the key elements and factors that affect adolescent mothers as they endure the pressures of early childbearing. Furthermore, these elements provide insight and guidance of teen mothers' perceptions, thoughts, and feelings of their emotional conquest of becoming a mother.

The theoretical assumptions for the study include psychosocial development posed by Erikson's (1968) psychosocial development theory and Kaiser and Hay's conceptual model (Erikson 1968; Kaiser and Hays 2004). Mercer's BAM theory was also used to examine the relationships between the themes and the similarities in the experiences of becoming a mother and developing maternal-role identity. The two themes related to Erikson's theory are conflicting identities and fluctuating emotions. Erikson's (1968) fifth stage—identity versus role confusion—was explored in the context of an adolescent mother's transition to motherhood.

Erikson characterized adolescent identity exploration as being a part of ego strength and cognitive restructuring, and the view of self is often the result of reduced ego strength and an impairment of coping (Kidwell et al. 1995). The dynamics of Erikson's concept of cognitive reconstructing was apparent in all twelve participants. This was evidenced by the participants' describing how they had begun the process of thinking before acting. They had also begun to make decisions beneficial to them and their children and to put the needs of their children first before their own. These were all examples of their cognitive reconstructing.

From a theoretical approach, Erikson's theory contends that the primary focus during adolescence is the development of a positive role identity formation (1963). After the adolescent completes his or her identity formation, the next stage is intimacy formation, which allows the adolescent to learn how to share himself or herself with another person as well as be in the position to maintain a sense of identity. When identity and intimacy are both achieved, the adolescent is ready for the generativity stage of parenting (1963). The concept of the positive role identity is based on adolescents' developing an understanding of themselves in the terms of their developmental achievements, aspirations, and expectations (Erikson 1963).

The conceptual model developed by Kaiser and Hays (2004) was used to display two themes that emerged from the data. Kaiser and Hays found that the success of an adolescent mother's transition is based on psychosocial factors that affect the transition itself. Kaiser and Hays identified four psychosocial factors that directly affect the transition: gaining acceptance, planning for the future, viewing self as a mother, and growing up. The two themes aligned with Kaiser and Hays's model were the emergence of a new and positive self and the constant need for support. There were many accounts from participants that exemplified the concepts from Kaiser and Hays's conceptual model.

The first component of the conceptual model is accepting that they are pregnant and will become mothers. The participants' responses to becoming pregnant included shock, worry, and feeling lost—but they all came to grips with the fact that they were going to be mothers and their lives would have to change.

Participant 4 shared that she was scared to tell her parents when she found out she was pregnant. Also, her boyfriend at the time was trying to convince her to get an abortion. She was able to accept her pregnancy after sharing the news with her mother and her telling her she was going to keep the baby:

> You know, like, no, and then, like, when I thought about it and after I told my mom, she was like, you're not getting no abortion. We're going to help you ... and, you know, so, I mean ... everything was good.

All twelve teen mothers described how their lives changed when they became mothers. They began making better decisions, putting their child's needs first, and thinking before acting.

The second component of the conceptual model is the act of planning for the future. Ten of the twelve participants discussed goals and plans concerning their futures. Another component of the model consists of the act of viewing themselves as mothers. Eight of the mothers adapted to their roles as mothers without experiencing conflicting role identity because they accepted their role as a mothers. Four mothers had to encounter high-risk situations—events that made them question their lifestyles and outcomes of their behaviors— before coming to grips with being mothers and their responsibility for another human being. Participant 1 was at party where she felt she could have lost her life. Participant 10 had emergency surgery that made her think about her child's life. Finally, participants 5 and 7 used drugs but then stopped when they became mothers.

The final component consists of the mothers' growing up, and they all revealed they have matured by becoming more responsible, changing their behaviors, and thinking before acting. Participant 8 described her process of recognizing the significant role she has to play. "I couldn't go out and live the party life anymore. I had big girl responsibilities. Couldn't spend my money on little stupid stuff anymore. I had to save my money." The concept of the maternal role definition was found to take place when the participants recognized they had to set aside their previous self-centered thoughts revolved around obtaining what they wanted and needed. They all remarked about a time or situation in which they had the cognitive thought and notion to feel the need to "put their child's needs first" and they could "no longer operate for themselves only." All twelve of the participants stated at least at once that they recognized being a mother required them to put their child's needs first and to leave behind some of their old ways of thinking.

The behaviors described by the participants in accordance with the conceptual model illustrate the personal processes in which they endured the emergence of a new and positive self. Participants 2, 4, 5, 6, 7,10, and 12 all shared that having their children ended their drug use, violent behavior, and other dangerous behaviors. Participant 10 provided her rationale for how she recognized she had to change because she was a mother:

> So me being a teen mother, I was going to be able to be no more wild fighting, and I would have to cut down on the partyin' or hangin' with friends. I have to more, focus on my child now I got somebody I have to I can raise and show what to do and what not to do.

Two of the participants mentioned no longer abusing narcotics because of becoming mothers. Rekindled relationships with mothers were also described in the emergence of self. Participant 5 referred to herself as a party animal, but she now considers herself to be drug free. She said, "I've calmed down a lot. I'm not doing drugs now, like I was before." Participant 7 stated she used to fall into a deep depression, and she would handle her depression by using crack.

Overall, the participants expressed self-satisfaction and were proud of themselves for beginning to make positive decisions beneficial not only to them but also to their child. They correlated the positive decision making to recognizing that they had become mothers.

Six themes emerged from this qualitative study: (a) experiencing conflicting identifies, (b) defining a new and positive sense of self, (c) accepting maternal role duties and responsibilities, (d) constantly needing support, (e) experiencing emotional cycling, and (f) experiencing mental health symptomology. Discussion of each theme is presented in the context of relevant and existing literature to highlight the relationship between the themes, theories, and existing literature.

Experiencing Conflicting Identities

The theme of experiencing conflicting identities was addressed in the context of Erikson's stage of adolescence when an adolescent is experiencing a crisis with his or her identity (Erikson 1963). The transitional process of becoming a mother caused the participants to experience many wavering emotions and interpersonal conflicts. With regard to the research question of how adolescent mothers describe their transition to motherhood, the majority of the participants reported being overwhelmed and confused about their roles as mothers. They appeared to emerge into a state of a psychological paradox of uncertainty after giving birth to their children. They described feeling conflicted between their roles of being a teen and becoming a mother.

They were aware they were adolescent, but they did not feel like they were; they weren't behaving as they once did, because of the new duties and responsibilities motherhood had thrust on them— thus causing conflicting identities. This relates to Erikson's concept of identity crisis, wherein society identifies who the adolescent has become and treats him or her accordingly. Erikson (1980) also contended that identity crisis demands a decisive and strategic repatterning of action (p. 123), which should be compromised by obtaining a society's value and increasing commitment. Therefore, adolescents can either recognize their identity and the roles thrust on them by society or reject it, therefore leaving them in what Erikson calls an *identity in crisis*. In the case of adolescent mothers, society's value was to endure the parental duties of a mother; however, the adolescent mothers selectively rejected those notions of being a parent because they still had teenage urges. For example, Participant 8 described this experience after sharing that her baby gave her a voice to speak up and defend herself; she still felt like a teen but had to think like an adult. Participant 6 explained how she did not know if she was able to be a mother, because she still considered herself to be a child.

> My anxiety was really high. I was nervous a lot. I didn't know if I was going to be able to be a mother. I still thought I was a child myself, and I didn't know how to take care of a baby. I didn't even know how to make a bottle so it was very, very hard for me. I was very scared.

Participant 12 described her experience of transitioning from being a teen to becoming to becoming mother as "awful." She said, "So it's just like me losing who I am and having to change into the one thing that I dislike the most was; it was hard. Like, it was awful. That's the only word I can use." She provided a more vivid example of why she felt the way she did about her experience. It was an example of her conflicting identities:

> And, it was godawful because, like, a normal teen is supposed to be like, *Okay, I can go to school, then I'm going to come home and chill with my friends. I'm going to have this party, I'm going to do these out-of-school activities,* where a teen mom has to, before you can go out to any party or before you can do anything, you have to make sure you've got a babysitter straight.

The emergence of the conflicting identities of adolescent and motherhood has been noted in previous studies. The central theme found with this study was the conflicting role identities—the wavering being teens and becoming mothers. Eight of the twelve participants discussed experiencing this wavering between the two worlds. They described it as having no clear understanding of their role as a mother because of feeling the urge and desire to engage in what is considered to be normal adolescent thoughts and behaviors.

Kaiser and Hays (2004) developed the terms *dual developmentalism* because they found adolescent mothers struggled with their developmental task of being an adolescent and having to learn to accept the new duties and responsibility as a mother. In addition, previous works from Salder and Catrone (1983), Clemmens (2002), and Breheny and Stephens (2007) found similar results in which adolescent mothers experienced identity conflicts in their adolescent identity construct and their maternal role construction. Participants 3 and 9 clearly stated they loved their children, but they wanted their lives back, their teen lives back. Participant 3 provided a depiction of this when she described the feeling of conflict. She said, "It was being at home with him was challenging because I was bored. I missed my friends. Some of my friends will be going late at night, and I'd be at home with a baby." The dual developmentalism was a noteworthy finding in this study because adolescent mothers are often expected to function and maintain their motherly duties and responsibilities as functioning adult mothers. They struggle, however, because cognitively they are not adults, and they cannot function as such (Borkowski 2007; McCrary and Weed 2005; Passino et al. 1993). The participants appeared to linger between the stages of identity and intimacy formation. This was apparent with the wavering notions of feeling forced into having to go from an egocentric persona to a more altruistic personality. The participants displayed this concept in two ways: struggling with the lost sense of identity and a willingness to sacrifice and share themselves with their children. Participant 2 provided an example; she stated that after having her child, she was no longer herself. "I am not me anymore," she said. She also described the point when she realized that she was a mother, and that was when she realized it was not about her anymore. "I guess the fact that it's not about me anymore. When I made decisions based on my son's needs and not mine, that's when it realized to me I was mom." The struggle with this concept of moving from an egocentric to a more altruistic personality was adamantly displayed with participant

12 when she was asked about her transition from being a teen to becoming a mother:

> I mean, I know there's like stuff that I am not supposed to do, and I know I got get it regardless of me being selfish. I know she had to have it, so of course I'm going to get it, but at the same, after I get out of bed, I'm like, well then, when's it going to be me time? When am I going to be able to get what I need? Every time I turn around, she needs something, but at end of the day, that shit bothers me that I am becoming a momma!

The inability of the adolescent mother to develop an autonomous sense of self (Brooks-Gun and Chase-Lansdale 1995) leaves her vulnerable and less likely to have the opportunity to develop her role identity adequately, whether self or parenting roles (Clemmens 2002; Hurlburt and McDonald 1997).

According to the dynamics of Erikson's theory (1963), the underdeveloped identity and developmental stages remaining in crisis put adolescent mothers' parenting at risk (Hurlburt and McDonald 1997; Noria et al. 2007. When the adolescent mother does not adjust to her new role and position of being a mother, she has a hard time adjusting to parenting and struggles for economic self-sufficiency (Noria et al. 2007).

Erikson's concept of role confusion was demonstrated by eighteen-year-old participant 9. When describing herself as a mother, she said,

> Well, I think I'm still—I'm still a teenager. But, um, I have to make adult decisions. So I mean it was, you know it was … it's kind of mixed. Like, um [feeling like an adult], sacrificing things for her.

When asked about challenges she faced during the transition, participant 3's response demonstrated the notion of having to be a mother but having the desire to be with friends.

> [At first] I don't know how to being mom. Being with my son, watching him grow up, actually growing up with him [was a challenge]. Not, you know, I'm always working. It was being at home with him was challenging because I was bored. I missed my friends.

Participant 11 was also sad about not being able to go out with her friends. She said, "But there was, like, sadness because it was like there were times when I wanted to go places ... and I couldn't just grab him up and go." Participant 4 recognized that she could not act on will with her friends asking her out. "Like, I couldn't just pick up and go when friends called, like, I was like, oh, well, let me see if I have a babysitter or sometimes it was like, no, I'm not going to go."

Overall, Erikson's (1968) concept of the identity crisis with the participants was apparent and prevalent in this study because of the participants' constant struggle between feeling the need to live up to societal obligations of being a responsible adult parent, yet fighting their own personal urges to behave like teenagers. Erikson contended that identity formation development is a process where an individual develops themselves in order of hierarchical roles step-by-step to a complete life span. The family, neighborhood, and school set the marker for adolescent experimental identification growth and development. Trying out different identities should bring about multiple identity options that give the adolescent an idea of what it would be like to be older and what it felt like to be younger. The expectations of these are verified step-by-step in decisive experiences; they become a part of the identity as determined by psychosocial "fittedness" (p. 123). In sum, the participants knew what responsibilities they had to undertake according to the societal role of motherhood, but they also felt the urge to engage in their teenage behaviors—socializing with friends, hanging out, and not having any other concerns but themselves.

Experiencing emotional cycling

Early childbearing places many burdens on adolescent mothers, especially when it comes to dealing simultaneously with the complexities of both motherhood and adolescence. All twelve participants spoke about fluctuating emotions and the cycling of emotions during their transitional process. The emotional cycling of being sad, happy, angry, and then sad again resonated with participants' descriptions. They recognized that they were mothers, making better choices and decisions for themselves and learning to put their children's needs first.

Research suggests it is common for first-time mothers to experience elevated levels of stress and depressive symptoms (Gaines et al. 2009; Lesser et al. 1999). The emotional cycling the adolescent mothers experience is common in early childbearing because of new responsibilities, different expectations, increased levels of anxiety and stress, and maternal identity negotiations (Abrams and Curran 2011). Many participants spoke about how their cycled feelings sometimes affected how they felt about having their children. They wished they had waited to have children or made better decisions for themselves; however, they were still happy to have had their children. For example, participant 2 shared her feelings about having her child:

> I wish that I was … just could've been more stable. If I just would've been more stable, things it would've been better. I guess just looking at him and when he smiles, it just changes, your heart melts completely. You can have your worst day ever, and just look like at your child, and it changes it … it makes it all better.

The fluctuation in the participants' moods appeared to derive from their immediate environments and their relationships with others in those environments. The participants' self-perceptions and the perceptions of others also had a direct effect on their moods. Nine of the twelve participants said that negative comments made by others caused them to have self-doubt and negative thoughts about themselves.

Kaye (2008) found that in adolescent mothers, early childbearing interfered with societal expectations of adolescents, their own educational and personal prospects, and their economic prospects. In addition, Lanzi et al. (2009) found lower-income adolescent mothers had significant stressors. These included lack of knowledge, minimal resources and having to deal with poverty-based issues, unstable environments, safety concerns, and increased violence—all of which the participants had experienced. Both studies correlated with the environmental factors affecting moods of the twelve participants (Kaye 2008; Lanzi et al. 2009). The situations in the participants' environments caused them great stress. Participants 1, 2, 5, 6, 7, 8, and 11 had issues with lack of stable housing during their transitions to motherhood. Participants 1 and 7 each had two children, and participant 7 also had an alcoholic father whom she cared for after he suffered a stroke. Their emotions varied and fluctuated, and they described feeling worried, anxious, nervous, scared, and uncertain. Participant 8 explained her stress as follows:

> Some of the stress was with my family. Some was my job. It was just mostly family and job. My dad, he wasn't … on the supportive side. He kicked me out the house. So I was basically living on the streets with my younger sister. I was very stressed out.

These feelings turned into frustration and anger. Participant 5 shared an example of this fluctuation. She said, "The angriness is, like I said, it was the frustration. Just, you know, anything that I let stay in my mind, let it get to me—that's mostly that. And me being happy is because of her." Participant 6 said this about her postpartum depression: "My postpartum was bad and caused me a lot of problems … I had no place to live, no job, always stressed me out and worrying and no one helped me, which pissed me off even more."

Postpartum depression has been found to be prevalent in adolescent mothers (Barnet et al. 2008; Clemmens 2002), specifically those who lack resources, have poor family structures, have minimal support, and experience elevated rates of stressors (Anderson 2008; Lanzi et al. 2009; Whitman et al. 2001). Two participants received treatment for their postpartum depression, whereas eight participants had symptoms of postpartum depression, similar to symptoms found in depression. Common feelings expressed by the participants two weeks after pregnancy included anxiety, irritation, tearfulness, and restlessness. Additional feelings included agitation or irritability, changes in appetite, feeling worthless or guilty, feeling withdrawn or disconnected, feeling a lack of pleasure or interest in most or all activities, loss of concentration, loss of energy, problems doing tasks at home or work, significant anxiety, thoughts of death or suicide, and trouble sleeping.

The negative perceptions of others was mentioned by several of the participants. However, they found solace within themselves and used the negative comments to motivate themselves to do the right things and make better choices. Participant 3 described how others rolled their eyes and made comments about her having her baby as a teen:

> I think teen moms need to be positive and not give up and not [let] people get us down and mad. Just know that we are somebody and we make mistakes, but my baby wasn't a mistake. I mean I love him to death, wasn't ready for him but I may be positive and not somebody negative that somebody to like bring you down.

Some participants felt angry and others felt sad when people made negative remarks about their early childbearing.

Adolescent mothers are often negatively stigmatized by family members, friends, and society (SmithBattle 2013). Some participants said that instead of allowing the issue of their early childbearing to affect them negatively in life, they chose to use their children as their motivation. Participant 7 said,

> You can only think about what's going on right now in the present. You say to yourself, *Your future's going to be all right.* You can always think about how, you know, how … *what am I going to do now to make sure my future's better?* So, it was like, you know, I just had to keep thinking everything that I was doing, I was doing this for the family.

As in previous studies with adolescent mothers (Clemmens 2002; Shanok and Miller 2007a; Wright and Davis 2008), participants were found to be resilient against the negative reactions toward their early childbearing. They did not allow the negative comments or the hard times to deter them from taking care of their children. They were resilient with their own feelings and emotions and found solace and inner strength to overcome the negative perceptions of others about their early childbearing. Participant 3 explained how seeing her baby's smiling face was a motivation for her, She said, "Yeah I guess you can say that was the motivation, because people around me brought me down all the time.

Defining a new and positive sense of self

The research literature is inundated with the negative outcomes of early childbearing in adolescent mothers, especially those living in urban environments (Bert et al. 2009; Borkowski, Whitman, and Farris 2007; Leadbeater and Way 2001; Lee 2009). However, although the participants in this study shared their hardships and personal dilemmas they encountered during their transitions to motherhood, all twelve of them found a new and positive self had emerged from their process. For instance, participant 1 found that being a mother was a positive experience for her because her biological mother had abandoned her. She said, "I had to teach myself to be a mom, because I didn't have any. So that was the most struggle, but good because it helped me grow and see myself positively."

From making better decisions and choices beneficial to their well-being to eliminating high-risk behaviors, to learning patience—the participants were visibly proud that having their children resulted in positive development for them. Participant 6 made changes immediately in going back to school:

> It depends which how you, which way you go, and I feel like she made me because she made me go the extra mile to do more things that I probably wouldn't even want. Like, I started school, but I dropped out and really didn't care—but now I'm back in school and I know it, that your mentor, that I have to finish school.

Participant 11 shared the fact that she had to stop being angry all the time, because people were trying to help her and her son:

> Sometimes you just got to take certain stuff, and, you know, certain stuff that you probably wouldn't take before having the baby. So basically just thinking about my child first, and you know, let everything else work out.

Participant 1 also spoke about the changes she made in how she handled things:

> I'm much calmer than I used to be. I used to be, you know, out there, and I'd be fighting, drinking, wildin' out, and since I had my kids, I have to think

about them. If I get hurt, how that going to affect them? What I do, my cause is going to affect them.

Brubaker and Wright (2006) found similar results in their narrative study conducted with fifty-one urban African American adolescent mothers. They reported participants experienced the personal growth of a new and positive identity, improved relationships, and a new commitment to maturity and responsibility.

Constantly needing support

The continual need for support was a theme mentioned by all participants. In all the interview responses, the lack of a particular element of support came up as either a relational or tangible item that hindered them and caused great strife during their transition. The common elements of support needed focused on emotional, financial, and social needs. All of the participants needed those key elements of support to assist them with their transitions to being mothers. In addressing research question #2—how adolescent mothers describe their transition from being teens to becoming mothers—a common element was the need for support.

The success of adolescent motherhood is fundamentally related to the amount of support the young mother has (Lodgson et al. 2008). Having the necessary resources and opportunities during the adolescent mother's transition has been identified as providing more favorable outcomes (Furstenberg 2007; Mollborn 2007; Oxford et al. 2010). The participants repeatedly spoke about the benefits of having support from their families, such as when participants 2, 4, 10, and 11 described how they had support from biological family members who helped them by providing housing, food, transportation, daycare, and emotional assistance with their transition. These participants reported feeling less stress about how to take care of themselves and their babies than the participants who did not have support. Taylor et al. (2012) found similar factors in his studies with urban African American adolescent mothers. When they had emotional support from their own families, they displayed more positive parenting toward their children. Additional research has shown that positive supportive actions from family equate to positive relationships, especially within African American families (Hess, Papas and Black 2002; Taylor et al. 2008, 2012).

Unfortunately, not all of the participants had the support of their family members. Participants 1, 5, 6, 7, 8, and 12 described their disadvantages of not having familial support and how that affected them emotionally and financially because they had to fend for themselves. In some cases, the mothers did not have a stable home environment, which caused them additional suffering and emotional discomfort. Other studies have shown a direct relationship between the adolescent mother's adjustment to parenting and increased of depression (Gee et al. 2003; Taylor et al. 2008, 2012).

Financial support was also a factor with the participants. With financial support, five of the participants described having their needs met, such as having enough diapers, formula, clothing, and childcare.

Employment was an issue for the participants, and nine of them spoke about the need to find a job so they could support their children. Five of the participants received federally-subsidized assistance, including food stamps and Temporary Assistance for Needy Families benefits. Unfortunately, the majority of the participants who were receiving federally-subsidized support fell into society's stereotype and stigma about young urban adolescent mothers (SmithBattle 2012). The stereotype that adolescent mothers are unmotivated, lazy, and have no desire or dreams for their future (SmithBattle 2013) was found to be false in the case of the twelve participants in this study. They spoke of completing school, finding stable housing for their children, and obtaining employment so they could provide for their children. All of the participants mentioned either a need for a job or wanting one.

Only one participant mentioned receiving support from a mentor, outside program, or organization for assistance. Participant 7 described how her mentor (her former teacher), helped motivate her and provide her with supportive services she was able to use to turn her life around. Sangalang (2006) found the use of case management frameworks to be successful in assisting adolescent mothers with their transitions to motherhood, due to the ability to incorporate multiple interventions, which they often lack. These included assistance with finishing their high school degrees, finding childcare and housing, obtaining jobs, or vocational assistance.

Finally, participants often mentioned the lack of social support. They shared their feelings about their loss of social support, especially the loss of relationships with their friends and their child's father. This loss of social support is a common experience of adolescent mothers during their transition (Saewyc 2003). They expressed feeling lonely, isolated, and even betrayed. Participants 1, 3, 6, and 11 discussed having emotions about their family making negative comments about them and not being there for them; these negative experiences motivated the participants to try harder to be successful. The low expectations— coupled with the negative comments—from others fueled them to want to persevere just to prove others wrong. Participant 5 shared her thoughts on the situation when she said, "You have a child young, you going to be labeled teen mom for the rest of your life, just part of the statistics for the rest of your life." She then provided a comment she uses as a motivational tool for herself:

> Believing in yourself and know that you want to get through, it may seem hard then but the sun will come up tomorrow—it's always going to be a brighter day. It's always going to be something better out there.

Participant 7 used positive thinking to help her combat the negative comments, glaring looks, and stereotyping from family and friends. Participant 1 provided a detailed description of her feelings about her family not being there for her.

> When I thought like I wasn't doing the best that I can do or when I felt like I couldn't get the help from my family, I would break down because I felt like

172

nobody was on my side. I felt alone and like betrayed by everybody and if … why couldn't I have help and ever be happy doing me?

Participant 11 spoke about the constant comments her family made about her. "Like your family always got something to say and an opinion about what you do, but then they don't do nothing for you," she said.

Five participants spoke about their friends losing contact with them, which left them feeling isolated and alone. These are common elements of peer interactions and engagements among adolescent mothers because their interests and responsibilities change after becoming parents (Hanna 2001; Levins 1995; Meadows-Oliver 2006). Participant 3 shared that it made her "mad" that she no longer hung out with her friends. "It was being at home with him was challenging because I was bored. I missed my friends!" she explained. "Some of my friends will be going late at night, and I'd be at home with a baby." Participant 6 also explained the process of how losing her friends was stressful for her.

> Like really not wanting to be involved— like some of my friends said before I was pregnant. Some of them are not my friends now because I have a baby, and I guess they feel I can't do the same things that they do now—which I still have a life, I still can do stuff, but I guess they feel like I can't. Um, I just tried to ignore it. Um, I care but I just always said I didn't care. Or it didn't matter to me.

The experience of feeling abandoned, ignored, and pushed aside by peers and family was found in previous research on adolescent mothers (Meadows-Oliver 2006). A meta-synthesis conducted on six qualitative studies of homeless, adolescent mothers revealed the following six themes replicated in all the studies: being homeless, enduring abuse, lamenting lost years, searching for support, recreating self, and seeking a better life (Meadows-Oliver 2006). All twelve participants in this study mentioned these topics when discussing their transition to motherhood.

The researcher found that many of the participants mentioned being abandoned, isolated, and shunned—and feeling lonely from family members and their peers (Meadows-Oliver 2006; Saewyc 2003).

Accepting maternal role duties and responsibilities

Issues around becoming a mother resonated with the twelve participants. They shared similar tales of being shocked when they first found out they were pregnant. Many were not prepared, and others learned to accept they were going to be mothers. Many of them shared that they first felt like a mother when they physically held their babies in their arms for the first time.

Participant 6 shared her experience of the moment reality sunk in for her about being a mother. "Like, when I was pregnant, I knew I had a baby in my stomach," she said. "It didn't seem real to me, when I had her, it was just like, *Oh, my god. I actually had a baby.*" They all knew they were mothers; however, they did not immediately assume their roles and responsibilities as mothers.

They toggled back and forth and questioned their roles as both mother and adolescent. Some participants were uncertain of their capability of being "good" mothers, whereas others looked for examples and role models to mimic because their mothers were not available—leaving them to develop their own concepts of motherhood. Erikson (1994) asserted that adolescents in a democratic country insist on self-made identities that enable them to grasp chances and be prepared to adjust to changing necessities of "boom and bust." This notion emphasizes the importance of autonomy in the form of independence and initiative, which Erikson referred to as a form of enterprise. The irony of the self-made identity is that the democratic system often neglects the self-made identities of millions of young Americans, because their upbringing and healthy development of personality depends on a degree of choice, hope for individual change, and certain conviction in freedom of self-determination (Erikson). Adolescent mothers are forced to create their own self-made identities. Being thrust into motherhood without support or guidance leaves them vulnerable to autocracy of conscience, which Erikson states is the cruel over-conscientiousness that is the inner residue of thoughts of the inequality bestowed on them with regards to their parent (1994). Erikson also stated that the loss of sense of identity exposes individuals to their own childhood conflicts. This notion was apparent with the adolescent mothers; when they needed assistance or guidance on how to parent, the repressed emotions and feelings about their mothers' parenting surfaced. Participants 1, 3, 6, 7, 8,10, and 12 all recalled moments or mentioned the lack of involvement or parental guidance from their mothers.

Mercer's BAM theory has also been recognized to occur in the participant's transition to developing the maternal-role identity.

Research question #1 addressed how teen mothers developed their maternal-role identity, and the participants had similar experiences regarding how they developed their identities, changed their behaviors, made changes in their decision making, put their children's needs first before theirs, and made their children a key element of positive motivation.

Participant 6 explained her challenge:

> I didn't have any patience before having my baby, and I had to teach myself to have more patience because she don't understand; she's just little. I need to be more understanding. She have needs that need to be met.

In addition, all of the participants recalled moments when they felt they had become mothers and when they started putting their child's needs before their own. They also spoke about learning to have patience and that this was a positive element and a change in their behavior that occurred with them becoming mothers.

Many of the participants eliminated their high-risk behaviors because they had become mothers. Eight of the twelve participants changed their high-risk behavior to serve as better role models and to put themselves in positions where they would still be able to take care of their children. They started to think about their children and the consequences of their actions—and how their actions affected their children.

Participant 1 said she had become calmer since becoming a mother and that she used to have a wild life. "I used to be, you know, out there," she said, "and I'd be fighting, drinking, wildin' out, and since I had my kids, I have to think about them." Mercer (2004) asserted that for a mother to achieve her maternal identity, she must go through the following steps: (a) establish a sense of commitment, attachment, and preparation during the pregnancy period; (b) go through a period of acquaintance, learning, and physical restoration during the first two to six weeks after birth; (c) move toward a new normal (two weeks to four months); and (d) finally achieve maternal identity (around four months; Mercer 2004). The stages can also overlap with one another. Data analysis of participants' responses showed that twelve of the participants experienced the first stage of the BAM theory, deciding to keep their children and then beginning to prepare to have their children.

The preparation process toward becoming a mother was more difficult for some teens than others. For example, six of the participants had to find stable housing for themselves and their children. They had to live with various individuals until they were able to receive income-based housing. Only one participant had a job while she was pregnant, and the remainder were seeking employment but finding it difficult because of transportation issues and lack of reliable daycare.

The second stage of acquaintance and learning for the participants varied depending on their levels of support. Some participants took longer to accept their roles as mothers because of stress, anxiety, and uncertainty; however, the learning process took effect immediately after their children came home. Mercer contended that during this stage the mother learns and practices comforting and caring for her child through trial and error.

The third stage was difficult for many of the participants, again because of the lack of support. This stage involves moving toward a new normal. Many of the participants did not have a stable environment to begin with; therefore, moving toward a "new normal" was very difficult for them.

Many were living in various locations and had different caretakers assisting them with their children. Not having stability made it difficult for them to establish their own independence, because there was a constant need of support from others. Eventually, however, each found her own sense of normalcy and began to build and plan according to what she had established for herself. The adolescent mothers were able to achieve this by recognizing that their roles and lives had changed and they were no longer able to do the things they did before having their children. This behavior is what Main and Hesse (1990) coined *disorganized attachment relationships,* which basically develop when children find themselves emotionally and physically dependent on someone who is also a source of fear or anxiety. This occurs under stressful conditions, which results in a paradoxical dilemma that breaks down the coping strategies. The disorganized attachment relationship can apply to adolescent mothers seeking support from members in their broken family relationships or their own children seeking support, attachment, and bonding from their mother. Similarly, Beers and Hollo (2009) found that understanding adolescent mothers' cooperative relationships and the dynamics of their environment can help practices in assisting adolescent mothers.

The fourth and final stage occurs within four months after the birth of the child. This stage consists of the mother experiencing a transformation in which she now views herself as a mother. Eleven of the twelve participants repeatedly said that they viewed themselves as mothers because of the changes in their behaviors and how they handled things in their new roles. Participant 12 revealed that she was "getting there" in accepting that she was an actual mother. She appeared to have discontent and disdain for her own biological mother, which affected her perception of motherhood; she referred to her child in terms of the things being taken away from her. She spoke about her life being taken from her and not understanding how her daughter has needs to be met:

> I mean, I know there's like stuff that I am not supposed to do, and I know I got get it regardless of me being selfish, I know she had to have it, so of course I'm going to get it, but at the same, after I get out of bed, I'm like, well then, when's it going to be me time? When am I going to be able to get what I need? Every time I turn around, she needs something, but at end of the day that shit bothers me that I am becoming a momma.

Participant 12 stated she had not fully grasped the concept of being a mother, because she still had thoughts about putting her needs before her child's with regard to material things, such as clothing. She explained, "I still don't think I'm a momma, because right now, let's say, for instance, I want a pair of shoes. I'm like, well, she need her shoes. I'm getting for me, like, I still debate back and forth." Her response is a common theme found in the literature with adolescent mothers who are struggling with maturation, egocentrism (Secco and Moffatt 2003), sensitivity to their child's needs (Salder and Cowlin 2003), and the maturational crisis of adolescence (Lodgson et al. 2008).

Overall, the participants developed their maternal-role identity through a pathway similar to that outlined in Mercer's BAM theory. The mothers experienced shock, uncertainty, and anxiety—and then finally acceptance—of their pregnancies. Then they began to plan. After giving birth, they experienced anxiety, uncertainty, and confusion, but then they developed attachment, became acquainted with their child, and experienced a learning process of the duties they needed to perform. They struggled with finding a sense of normalcy, but they all had situations, All but one participant ultimately accepted and embraced her role as a mother.

Brubaker and Wright (2006) also found in urban adolescent mother narratives an acceptance of their roles as mothers and a process that was a positive experience for their "negatively deemed" action of early childbearing. These positive effects on adolescent mothers—such as helping them deter negative behaviors, becoming more responsible, and being a positive solution for some of traumatic life trajectories, like failure to complete high school, unemployment, and unstable housing—have been found in numerous studies (Furstenberg 2007; Jacobs and Mollborn 2012; Lesser et al. 2003; Milan et al. 2004; Salder and Cowlin 2003; Shanok and Miller 2007b; SmithBattle and Leonard 2012; Wright and Davis 2008).

Experiencing mental health symptomology

The participants expressed feeling "depressed" throughout their transitional process. In fact, they described experiencing an array of clinical symptomologies, ranging from feeling depressed to experiencing high levels of anxiety.

Adolescent mothers have been found to have an increased risk for psychological problems (Knoche et al. 2007; Mayberry, Horowitz, and De Clercq 2007), and they tend to have a great deal of stress and socio-emotional maladjustment (Borkowski et al. 2002). Seven of the participants reported feeling "depressed," whereas two were receiving treatment and were prescribed medication for their postpartum depression. Participant 7 described having physical side effects from her depression:

> But I was always like crying, worried. It hurt or whatnot, so I went through a lot of like physical changes. Just had a lot of migraine headaches. Sometimes I won't want to get out of bed. I was so depressed, and my body just wouldn't function right.

Knoche and colleagues (2007) found that adolescent mothers experience postpartum depression at much higher rates than adult women. First-time adolescent mothers have significantly higher depressive symptoms than first-time adult mothers (Schmidt et al. 2006; Whitman et al. 2001). Birkeland et al. (2005) found that 29 percent of the adolescent mother participants experienced symptoms of clinical depression. Boden et al. (2008) found that early motherhood was associated with higher levels of mental health disorders, lower levels of educational achievement, and higher levels of welfare dependency.

Two of the participants mentioned they were diagnosed with Bipolar disorder (Participant 1 mentioned this during her interview, and participant 6 mentioned it after the interview). Participants 5 and 7 had both mentioned being drug abusers before they become mothers, and all but two participants mentioned they had to stop "drinking or partying" with friends or mentioned ending any high-risk behaviors after becoming mothers. The participants did not mention their levels of coping with their depression, which is a definite topic for further study. Most of them seem to have experienced significant levels of postpartum depression symptoms.

The increased levels of depression were related to the low levels of support Participants 2, 4, 10, 11, and 12 had consistent and continuous assistance and experienced feelings of anxiety of worry about how to care for the baby; they felt overwhelmed at times about their new duties and responsibilities.

They also mentioned feeling upset about the loss of their social contact with friends, but they did not mention feeling depressed. The remaining participants (1, 3, 5, 6, 7, 8, and 9) who had less support from family repeatedly expressed their feelings of depression, anxiety, sadness, anger, and frustration.

Common factors of single parenthood and urban living often leave individuals with the mixed emotions of high anxiety and depression (Taylor 2011). The participants discussed their mixed emotions of anger, depression, sadness, and anxiety. Easterbrooks et al. (2010) found similar results in their study conducted on urban adolescent mothers. Taylor (2011) found that when urban adolescent mothers lacked the necessary resources and support, they experienced increased levels of psychological stress, which affected their parenting. Similarly, adolescent mothers have been experiencing postpartum depression and clinical depression that has gone untreated (Barnet et al. 2008). Four of the participants who received support from their biological mothers and family members did not mention feeling depressed, but they mentioned experiencing anxiety and uncertainty.

Postpartum depression has been found to be higher in adolescent mothers compared with (older) adult mothers (Nunes and Phipps 2012). In addition, Anderson (2008) found that adolescent mothers describing their postpartum depression have said they felt isolated, alone, and abandoned. This further supports the notion that adolescent mothers need support systems to assist them with their transition (Anderson 2008). Untreated postpartum depression often leads to broader issues as the mother further undertakes her duties and responsibilities; these issues include poor parenting practices (Borkowski et al. 2002) and attachment issues (Stiles 2010). These were significant hurdles for participant 12, who discussed how hard it was for her to bond with her child because of not wanting to share herself with anyone. Barnet et al. (2008) also found maternal depression is associated with interpersonal conflicts and risks of child abuse and neglect, which can affects the child's development. Five of the twelve participants who were in foster care spoke about being a good mother so their child would not get taken from them. It was apparent they understood the necessity of positive parenting.

Implications for Practice

Twelve urban adolescent mothers shared their experiences of transitioning from being a teen to becoming a mother. The recurrence of responses pertaining to the concept of needing and requiring support was noted as an overwhelming factor that emerged from all twelve participants. The need for emotional, financial, and social support came up frequently in the participants' transcripts. They said several times that with more support or resources, they would have had a better transitional experience.

The transition to motherhood revealed many emotions and cognitive and behavioral changes. The emotional cycling and psychological paradox the mothers experienced revealed the need for mental health assistance. The mixed feelings of being a mother and wanting to remain a teenager fueled a constant emotional battle for the participants. Feeling sad, angry, happy, and sad again was a cycle felt by all of participants. Seven of them experienced postpartum depression. Two recognized the need for help with their postpartum depression and sought treatment, which they reported helped them.

The cycling of emotions also included the back and forth of varying emotions such as feeling alone, abandoned, and isolated by friends, family, and their community—and then feeling happy, elated, and satisfied about having their child and the joy and positive effect it had on their lives. The cycles continued with anger, anxiety, and irritation, which led to agitation, frustration, resentment, and—in some cases—a sense of vengefulness toward their situation and toward those they felt caused the pain. This example of emotional cycling was apparent in most of the participants. Previous studies have found similar behaviors, revealing a similar emotional process that adolescent mothers engage in during this transitional period of being a teen and becoming a mother (Reid and Meadows–Oliver 2007; Secco et al. 2007; Sommer et al. 2000).

More educational literature and programming in urban areas would be beneficial to stress the importance of awareness and intervention of postpartum depression in adolescent mothers.

Abrams and Curran (2011) found similar behaviors in a study conducted on low-income women and the symptoms of postpartum depression. In addition to providing nursing and clinical practitioners to adolescent mothers, supportive services such as parenting groups, classes, educational seminars, and workshops should be provided in common places they naturally engage. Eight of the participants mentioned the benefits of having a home nursing program, mentor, or reading material to get a better understanding of parenting. All twelve participants revealed there were times they felt isolated, uncertain as to what to do, ashamed, alone, and abandoned— all feelings that resonate with the adolescent mother population.

Recommendations for Adolescent Mothers

Adolescent mothers need support, guidance, nurturing, and stability to assist with their transition to motherhood (Jacobs and Mollborn 2012; SmithBattle 2013). Community-based home visiting programs should include modules with practices that incorporate strength-based interventions due to the lack of self-confidence, low self-efficacy, and poor self-perceptions for this population (Barnet et al. 2008; Black et al. 2006). Strength-based interventions could assist in enhancing the adolescent mother's self-esteem and bolster her self-confidence, so she will be willing and open to receiving the guidance and direction she needs, instead of being defensive and uncooperative because of mixed feelings of shame and lack of knowledge (Cox et al. 2008; Reid and Meadows-Oliver 2007). The programming should also include modules that enhance adolescent mothers' critical thinking and analytical skills. This would enable to them to learn to effectively cognitively process issues that arise and not resort to acting and responding impulsively, which urban adolescents often do when they feel they have to protect themselves (Rolfe 2008; Shanok and Miller 2005; Taylor 2011)

Emotional cycling has been found to be an intricate part of the transitional process for adolescent mothers. It appears to fuel the psychological paradox, which is a state to which adolescent mothers ruminate emotionally and mentally over the inconsistent thoughts of their roles as both adolescents and mothers (Noria et al. 2007).

Adolescent mothers are torn between their emotions and feelings, which are displayed in their behaviors. The impulsiveness and egocentric thinking that leads to irrational thinking are basic behaviors of adolescence (Cox et al. 2008; Noria et al. 2007).

Recommendations for Future Research

Previously research on the welfare of urban adolescent mothers as they transitioned to their roles as mothers have been quantitative or have primarily focused on the negative outcomes pertaining to their results of their children or the mental health of the mother (Ammerman et al. 2012; Rosengard et al. 2006; Sumner et al. 2012).

The research is inundated with reports of abuse or neglect of children, depression, violence, and lack of educational obtainment (Coley and Chase-Lansdale 1998; Driscoll et al. 2005; Furstenberg et al. 1987; Henretta 2007; Taylor 2010; Whitman et al. 2001).

However, this study used a qualitative phenomenological approach to gain an understanding of the experiences of urban teens as they transitioned into mothers and developed their maternal role identities. The sample of urban teens provided a better understanding of the true essences that exist as urban adolescent mothers transition into their roles as mothers. Few studies have explored the transitional aspects of being a teen and then becoming a mother, presenting a gap in the research. This study addressed the gap in the literature, and new ideas and concepts emerged from the findings that require further research. The new ideas and concepts include the emotional cycling experienced by adolescent mothers, the psychological paradox in which they find themselves toggling between being a teen and accepting their roles as mothers, and early childbearing as a positive aspect and component in their lives. Additional research is needed on other samples from different geographic areas or ethnic/racial backgrounds. Furthermore, additional research is needed to develop interventions and strategies that would assist the adolescent mothers with their transition to becoming mothers and understanding their new duties and responsibilities (Cronin 2003; Sadler Swartz et al. 2007; SmithBattle 2007, 2012),

Previous studies have addressed the need for additional research pertaining to the transitional process undertaken by adolescent mothers during their adolescent stage of development (Hurlburt and McDonald 1997; Kaye 2008; Shanok and Miller 2007b). To fully gain knowledge of the frameworks within adolescent mothers' development into their roles as mothers, an understanding of the psychosocial factors must be addressed and understood (Hurlburt and McDonald 1997; Jaffee et al. 2001; Xie, Cairns, and Cairns 2001). Understanding the effects of psychosocial factors on the cognitive perceptions of adolescent mothers should help determine which elements, if any, have a direct impact on or influence these changes in adolescent mothers. These issues are vital to understanding the adolescent mother's evolution into her role, because of the known outcomes of not having the necessary support, programming, and services needed to achieve a healthy transition (Letourneau et al. 2004; SmithBattle 2007). Therefore, future qualitative research should be conducted to capture the essence of the transitional process from a larger scope of adolescent mothers from the standpoint of age, geographical regions, and varying ethnic groups (SmithBattle 2012).

Finally, Erikson's psychosocial development theory was used to understand what teen mothers endure and experience during their adolescent stage of development. The participants were heavily influenced by many underlying systems in their communities, including family, school, neighborhoods, peers, and interpersonal relationships. A further study using more system-based theories—such as Brofeinbrenner's bioecological system—could be ideal to capture the influences that the multiple systems have on the transitional process. Previous studies using the systems theory approach were able to obtain data from different influences by exploring the multiple ecological factors that contribute to the development of personality and parenting. This enabled them to draw conclusions from various aspects (Meade et al. 2008; Ramey et al. 2000).

Further study on the transition to becoming a mother would shed light on the process that adolescent mothers use to establish their own concepts of home, family, and mothering.

Understanding how adolescent mothers come to stabilize and become mothers would contribute to the human services field because knowing the key factors and elements would enable a proactive intervention to assist adolescent mothers with their transitional process.

CONCLUSION

The purpose of this phenomenological study was to understand the transitional process of becoming a mother for urban adolescent mothers and to understand how they develop their maternal role identities. The results from this research provide a defined understanding of the perceptions, thoughts, feelings, and experiences of urban adolescent mothers as they transition from being teens to being mothers. In addition, this study establishes an understanding of the psychosocial effects of early childbearing and their impact on the adolescent mother's dual development of self-identity and maternal identity—and how they affect her ability to parent.

With the use of a phenomenological approach, twelve urban adolescent mothers ages eighteen to twenty-two volunteered to be interviewed and to share and discuss the true essences of their experiences as they transitioned from being teens to becoming mothers. The twelve participants provided insight on their transitional process, and six nomothetic themes emerged from the data analysis: (a) experiencing conflicting identities, (b) defining a new and positive sense of self, (c) accepting maternal role duties and responsibilities, (d) constantly needing support, (e) experiencing emotional cycling, and (f) experiencing mental health symptomology. The results of this study also revealed additional factors that adolescent mothers endure as they transition into their roles as mothers. The adolescent mothers revealed experiencing a cycling of their emotions, which they described as feeling, sad, happy, angry, lonely, and so forth all at the same time. The cycling of emotions was experienced in episodes of feeling sad or low and then immediately feeling happy or high. Then additional thinking caused feelings to shift back down to low and then finish off with a balance of being resentful or feeling a sense of hopelessness.

The emotional cycling appeared to fuel their perceptions of the psychological paradox to which the adolescent mothers would ruminate emotionally and mentally over the inconsistent cognitive perceptions of their roles as adolescents or mothers. Kaiser and Hays (2004) referred to this phenomenon as dual developmentalism. In either case, the adolescent mothers were torn between their emotions and feelings of who and what they were and inconsistencies in their thinking displayed in their behaviors.

Additional research should investigate the emotional and perceptual processes endured by adolescent mothers to determine the cycles they complete to accept themselves as mothers. The psychological paradox—dueling identities of teen and mother—is another concept that requires further investigation to determine the effects on the adolescent mothers' mental state and parenting duties. The study also revealed an additional level of awareness of how teen pregnancy—although deemed as having a negative impact on adolescent mothers in today's society—ironically served to have a positive impact on the mothers who revealed being involved previously with high-risk behaviors. The participants' recounting of their transitions to motherhood were filled with rich descriptions of triumph and resilience. They provided insights on how the birth of their children—even though at an inopportune time—served as a catalyst to end their high-risk behaviors (such as drinking, high-risk sexual behaviors, drug use, street violence, and reckless endangerment). Their children were a reason for many of them to put an end to those behaviors and instead strive for a life filled with positivity, goal setting, and positive role modeling.

References

Abrams, L. S., and L. Curran. 2011. "Maternal identity negations among low-income women with symptoms of postpartum depression." *Qualitative Health Research* 21 (3): 373–385.

Aiello, R., and S. Lancaster. 2007. "Influence of adolescent maternal characteristics on infant development." *Infant Mental Health Journal* 28 (5): 496–516. doi:10.1002/imjh.20150.

Aisenberg, E., and K. Ell. 2005. "Contextualizing community violence and its effects: an ecological model of parent-child interdependent coping." *Journal of Interpersonal Violence* 20 (7): 855–871.

Alan Guttmacher Institute. 2004. "US teenage pregnancy statistics. Overall trends, trends by race and ethnicity, and state-by-state information." https://www.guttmacher.org/pubs/state_pregnancy_trends.pdf

Ammerman, R. T., F. W. Putnam, J. Stevens, K. M. Chard,, and J. B. Van Ginkel. 2012. "PTSD in depressed mothers in home visitation." *Psychological Training Theory, Research, Practice, and Policy* 4 (2): 186–195.

Anderson, C. 2008. "Psychological consequences of childbirth among adolescents. *Nurses' Lounge* (April): 22–26.

Anthony, E. K. 2008. "Cluster profiles of youths living in urban poverty: Factors affecting risk and resilience." *Social Work Research* 32 (1): 6–17.

Barker, R., ed. 2009. *Making sense of every child matters: Multi-professional practice guide.* Portland, OR: Policy Press.

Barratt, M. S., M. A. Roach, K. M. Morgan, and K. K.Colbert. 1996. "Adjustment to motherhood by single adolescents." *Family Relations* 45 (2): 209– 215.

Barnet, B., J. Liu, and M. DeVoe. 2008. "Double jeopardy: Depressive symptoms and rapid subsequent pregnancy in adolescent mothers." *Archives of Pediatrics and Adolescent Medicine* 162 (3): 246–252.

Bartlett, J. D., and M. Easterbrooks, M. 2012. "Links between physical abuse in childhood and child neglect among adolescent mothers." *Children and Youth Services Review* 34 (11): 2164–2169. http://dx.doi.org/10.1016/j.childyouth.2012.07.011.

189

Beauchamp, T. L., and J. F. Childress. 2009. *Principles of Biomedical Ethics* (6ᵗʰ ed.). Oxford, UK: Oxford University Press.

Benson, M. 2004. After the adolescent pregnancy: Parents, teens, and families." *Child and Adolescent Social Work Journal* 21 (5): 435–454.

Beers, L. A. S., and R. E. Hollo. 2009. "Approaching the adolescent-headed family: A review of teen parenting." *Current Problems in Pediatric and Adolescent Health Care* 39 (9): 216–233.

Bert, S. C., B. M Guner, and R. G. Lanzi. 2009. "The influence of maternal history of abuse on parenting knowledge and behavior." *Family Relations* 58(2), 176–187.

Birkeland, R., J. K. Thompson, and V. Phares. 2005. "Adolescent motherhood and postpartum depression." *Journal of Clinical Child and Adolescent Psychology* 34: 292–300.

Black, C., and M. Ford-Gilboe. 2004. "Adolescent mothers: Resilience, family health work, and health-promoting practices." *Journal of Advanced Nursing* 48 (4): 351–360.

Black, M. M., M. E. Bentley, M. A Papas, S. Orberlander, L. O Teti, S. McNary, and M. O. O'Connell. 2006. "Delaying second births among adolescent mothers: A randomized controlled trial of a home-based mentoring program." *Pediatrics* 118 (4): 1087–1099.

Blocher, D. H. 2000. *Counseling: A Developmental Approach* (4ᵗʰ ed.) New York, NY: Wiley.

Bloomberg, L. D., and M. Volpe. 2008. *Completing Your Qualitative Dissertation.* Thousand Oaks, CA: Sage.

Boden, J. M., D. M. Fergusson, and L. J. Horwood. 2008. "Early motherhood and subsequent life outcomes." *Journal of Child Psychology and Psychiatry,* 49 (2): 151–160. doi:10.1111/j.1469-7610.2007.01830.x

Booth, A., E. Rustenbach,, and S. McHale. 2008. "Early family transitions and depressive symptom changes from adolescence to early adulthood." *Journal of Marriage and Family* 70: 3–14. doi:10.1111/j.1741- 3737.2007.00457.x

Borkowoski, J. G., T. L. Whitman, and J. R. Farris. 2007. "Adolescent mothers and their children: Risks, resilience, and development." In J. G. Borkowoski, J. R, Farris, T. L. Whitman, S. S, Carothers, K. Weed, and D. A. Keogh (eds.). *Risk and Resilience: Adolescent Mothers and Their Children Grow Up* (pp. 1–34). Mahwah, NJ: Erlbaum.

Borkowski, J. G., Whitman, T. L., and D. A. Keogh. 2007. Toward resilience: Designing effective prevention programs. In J. G. Borkowoski, J. R. Farris, T. L. Whitman, S. S. Carothers, K. Weed, and D. A. Keogh, eds. *Risk and Resilience: Adolescent Mothers and Their Children Grow Up* (pp. 36–67). Mahwah, NJ: Erlbaum.

Bornstein, M. H., and D. L. Putnick. 2007. "Chronological age, cognitions, and practices in European American mothers: A multivariate study of parenting." *Developmental Psychology* 43 (4): 850.

Boyce, M. 1993. "Female psychological development: A model and implications for counselors and educators." In Hayes, R., and R. Aubrey (eds.), *New Directions for Counseling and Human Development*. Denver, CO: Love.

Breheny, M., and C. Stephens. 2007. "Irreconcilable differences: Health professionals' constructions of adolescent and motherhood." *Social Science and Medicine* 64: 112–124.

Brien, M. J., and R. J. Willis. 1997. "Costs and consequences for the fathers." In S.D. Hoffman and Maynard, R. A., eds., *Kids Having Kids: Economic Costs and Social Consequences of Teen Pregnancy* (pp. 95–144). Washington, D.C.: Urban Institute Press.

Brockenbrough, K. K., D. G. Cornell, and A. B. Loper. 2002. "Aggressive attitudes among victims of violence at school." *Education and Treatment of Children* 25 (3): 273.

Brooks-Gunn, J., and P. L. Chase-Lansdale. 1995. "Adolescent parenthood." In J. Brooks-Gunn, P. L. Chase-Lansdale, and M. H. Bornstein, eds., *Handbook of Parenting: Status and Social Conditions of Parenting* (Vol. 3, pp. 113–149). Hillsdale, NJ: Erlbaum.

Budd, S. K., M. J. A. Holdsworth, and K. D. HoganBruen. 2006. "Antecedents and concomitants of parenting stress in adolescent mothers in foster care." *Child Abuse and Neglect* 30: 557–574. doi:10.1016/j.chiabu.2005.11.006.

Burton, L. 2007. "Childhood adultification in economically disadvantaged families: A conceptual model." *Family Relations* 56: 329–345. doi:10.1111/j.1741-3729.2007.00463.x.

Caldwell, C. H., T. C. Antonucci, and J. S. Jackson. 1998. "Supportive/conflictual family relations and depressive symptomatology: Teenage mother and grandmother perspectives." *Family Relations* 47 (4): 395–402.

Chang, Y., and M. A. Fine. 2007. "Modeling parenting stress trajectories among low-income young mothers across the child's second and third years: Factors accounting for stability and change." *Journal of Family Planning* 21 (4): 584–594.

City of Richmond Health Department. 2012. Richmond Campaign to Prevent Teen Pregnancy. http://www.vdh.virginia.gov/LHD/richmondcity/richmondcampaign/

Clemmens, D. A. 2002. "Adolescent mothers' depression after the birth of their babies: Weathering the storm." *Adolescence* 37 (147): 551–565.

———. 2003. "Adolescent motherhood: A meta-synthesis of qualitative studies." *The American Journal of Maternal/Child Nursing* 28 (2): 93–99.

Cohen, L., L. Manion, and K. Morrison. 2007. *Research Methods in Education* (6th ed.) London, U.K.: Routledge.

Coley, R. L., and P. L. Chase-Lansdale. 1998. "Adolescent pregnancy and parenthood: Recent evidence and future directions. *American Psychologist* 53 (2): 152.

Copeland, D. B., and B. L. Harbaugh. 2010. "Psychosocial differences related to parenting infants among single and married mothers." *Issues in Comprehensive Pediatric Nursing* 33 (3): 129–148.

Corbin, J., and A. Straus,. eds. 2008. *Basics of Qualitative Research: Techniques and Procedures for Developing Grounded Theory.* Los Angeles, CA: Sage.

Corcoran, C., C. Franklin, and P. Bennett. 2000. "Ecological factors associated with adolescent pregnancy and parenting." *Social Work Research* 24 (1): 29–39.

Corcoran, M. E., and J. P. Kunz. 1997. "Do unmarried births among African-American teens lead to adult poverty? *The Social Service Review* 71 (2): 274–287.

Cox, J. E., M. Buman, J. Valenzuela, N. P. Joseph, A. Mitchell, and E. R. Woods. 2008. "Depression, parenting attributes, and social upport among adolescent mothers attending a teen tot program." *Journal of Pediatric and Adolescent Gynecology* 21 (5): 275–281.

Crawford, T., P. Cohen, J. G. Johnson, J. R. Sneed, and J. S. Brooks. 2004. "The course and psychosocial correlates of personality disorder symptoms in adolescence: Erikson's Developmental Theory revisited." *Journal of Youth and Adolescence* 33 (5): 373–387.

Creswell, J. W. 1998. *Qualitative Inquiry and Research Design.* Thousand Oaks, CA: Sage.

———. 2007. *Qualitative Inquiry and Research Design: Choosing Among Five Approaches.* Thousand Oaks, CA: Sage.

———. 2009. *Research Design: Qualitative, Quantitative, and Mixed Methods Approaches.* Thousand Oaks, CA: Sage. Creswell, J. W., and D. L. Miller. 2000. "Determining validity in qualitative inquiry." *Theory into Practice* 39 (3): 124-130.

Cronin, C. 2003. First-time mothers—identifying their needs, perceptions and experiences. *Journal of Clinical Nursing* 12 (2): 260–267.

Davis, A. A., J. E. Rhodes, and J. Hamilton-Leaks. 1997. "When both parents may be a source of support and problems: An analysis of pregnant and parenting female African American adolescents' relationships with their mothers and fathers." *Journal of Research on Adolescence* 7 (3): 331– 348.

Deal, L. W., and V. L. Holt,.1998. "Young maternal age and depressive symptoms: Results from the 1988 National Maternal and Infant Health Survey." *American Journal of Public Health* 8: 266–270.

Denzin, N. K., and Y. S. Lincoln, eds. 1994. *Handbook of qualitative research.* Thousand Oaks, CA: Sage.

_____. 2003. *Collecting and interpreting qualitative materials.* (2nd ed.). Thousand Oaks, CA: Sage.

US Department of Commerce, Census Bureau. 2011. "Urban area criteria for the 2010 Census; Notice." *Federal Register* 76 (164): 53030–53043. http://www.gpo.gov/fdsys/pkg/FR-2011-08-24/pdf/2011- 21647.pdf.

DeSocio, J. E., M. L. Holland, H. J. Kitzman, and R. E. Cole. 2013. "The influence of social-developmental context and nurse visitation intervention on self-agency change in unmarried adolescent mothers." *Research in Nursing and Health* 36 (2): 158–170. doi:10.1002/nur.21525. Deutscher, B., R. R. Fewell, and M. Gross. 2006. "Enhancing the interactions of teenage mothers and their at risk children; effectiveness of a maternal- focused intervention." *Topics of Early Childhood Special Education* 26 (4): 194–205.

Devito, J. 2007. "Self-perceptions of parenting among adolescent mothers." *The Journal of Perinatal Education* 16 (1): 16–23.

Driscoll, A. K., B. Sugland, J. Manlove, and A. R. Papillo. 2005. "Community opportunity, perceptions of opportunity, and the odds of an adolescent birth." *Youth and Society* 37: 33–61. doi:10.1177/0044118X04267493.

Drummond, J. E., N. Letourneau, S. M. Neufeld, M. Stewart, and A. Weir. 2008. "Effectiveness of teaching an early parenting approach within a community-based support service for adolescent mothers." *Research in Nursing and Health* 31: 12–22.

Dunn, B. H. 2008. *Unmarried childbearing: Fragile relationships, costly consequences.* Richmond, VA: The Community Foundation. Final report. http://www.tcfrichmond.org/images/uploads/Unmarried_Childbearing_F inal_Report.pdf

Easterbrooks, M. A., J. H. Chaudhuri, J. D. Bartlett, and A. Copeman. 2010. "Resilience in ecological risks and opportunities." *Children and Youth Services Review* 9: 1–9.

Easterbrooks, M. A., J. H. Chaudhuri, S. Gestsdottir. 2005. "Patterns of emotional availability among young mothers and their infants: A dyadic, contextual analysis." *Infant Mental Health Journal* 26: 309–326. doi:10.1002/imhj.20057.

Edin, K., and M. Kefalas. 2005. *Promises I can keep: Why poor women put motherhood before marriage.* Berkeley: University of California Press.

Edwards, R. C., M. J. Thullen, N. Isarowong, C. S. Shiu, L. Henson, S. L. Hans. 2012. "Supportive relationships and the trajectory of depressive symptoms among young African American mothers." *Journal of Family Psychology,* 26 (4): 585–594. doi:10.1037/a0029053.

Eghan, A. D. 2007. "Facilitating the Adolescent Mother's Transition to Motherhood: A Hermeneutical Approach." Unpublished doctoral dissertation, Capella University, Minneapolis, MN.

Erikson, E. H. 1959. *Young Man Luther: A Study in Psychoanalysis and History.* London, UK: Faber.

———. 1963. *Childhood and Society* (2nd ed.). New York, NY: Norton.

———. 1968. *Identity: Youth and Crisis* (No. 7). New York, NY: Norton.

———. 1994. *Insight and Responsibility*. New York, NY: Norton.

———. 1980. *Identity and the Life Cycle* (Vol. 1). New York, NY: Norton.

Eshabugh, E. M., J. Lempers, and G. Luze. 2006. "Objective and self-perceived resources as predictors of depression among urban and non-urban adolescent mothers." *Youth Adolescence* 35: 839–847.

Eshbaugh, E. 2006. "Predictors of depressive symptomatology among low-income adolescent mothers." *Archives of Women's Mental Health* 9 (9): 339–342.

Eshbaugh-Soha, M., and J. Peake. 2011. *Breaking through the noise: Presidential leadership, public opinion, and the news media*. Stanford, CA: Stanford University Press.

Eth, S., and R. S. Pynoos. 1994. "Children who witness the homicide of a parent."

Psychiatry: Interpersonal and Biological Processes 57 (4): 287–306.

Flanagan, P. J., M. M. McGrath, E. C. Meyer, and C. T. Coll. 1995. "Adolescent development and transitions to motherhood." *Pediatrics* 96 (2): 273– 277.

Florsheim, P., E. Sumida, C. McCann, M. Winstanley, R. Fukui, T. Seefeldt, and D. Moore. 2003. "The transition to parenthood among African-American and Latino couples: Relational predictors of risk for parental dysfunction." *Journal of Family Psychology* 17: 65–79.

Fouquier, K. F. 2011. "The concept of motherhood among three generations of African American women." *Journal of Nursing Scholarship* 43 (2):145–153.

Furstenberg, F. F. 2003. "Teenage childbearing as a public issue and private concern." *Annual Review of Sociology* 29: 23–29.

Furstenberg, F. F., J. Brooks-Gunn, and S. P. Morgan. 1987. "Adolescent mothers and their children in later life." *Family Planning Perspectives* 19 (4): 142–151.

Furstenberg, F. F., M. E. Hughes, and J. Brooks-Gunn. 1993. "The next generation: The children of teenage mothers grow up." In M. K. Rosenheim and M. F. Testa (Eds.), *Early parenthood and the coming of age in the 1990s* (pp. 113–135). New Brunswick, NJ: Rutgers University Press.

Furstenberg, F. F. 2007. *Destinies of the Disadvantaged: The Politics of Teen Childbearing*. New York, NY: Russell Sage Foundation.

Gaines, R., S. C. Bert, and B. K. Jacobs. 2009. "Depression among a sample of first-time adolescent and adult mothers." *Journal of Child and Adolescent Psychiatric Nursing* 22 (4): 194–202.

Garza, G. 2005. *The science of qualitative research: Validity and reliability reframed in terms of meaning.* http://www.iiqi.org/C4QI/httpdocs/qi2005/papers/garza.pdf

Gee, C. B., M. J. Nicholson, L. N. Osborne, and J. E. Rhodes. 2003. "Support and strain in pregnant and parenting adolescents' sibling relationships." *Journal of Adolescent Research* 18 (1): 25–35.

Geronimus, A. T. 2003. "Damned if you do: Culture, identity, privilege, and teenage childbearing in the United States." *Social Science and Medicine* 57 (5): 881–893.

Geronimus, A. T., and S. Korenman. 1992. "The socioeconomic consequences of teen childbearing reconsidered." *The Quarterly Journal of Economics* 107 (4): 1187–1214.

Giorgi, A., ed. 1985. *Phenomenology and Psychological Research*. Pittsburgh, PA: Duquesne University Press.

Giorgi, A. 2009. *The Descriptive phenomenological method in psychology: A modified Husserlian approach*. Pittsburgh, PA: Duquesne University Press.

Goodman, G., and L. J. Aber. 2010. "Predictors of representational aggression in preschool children of low-income urban African American adolescent mothers." *Infant Mental Health Journal,* 3 (1): 33–57. doi:10.1002/imhj.20241.

Grix, J. 2004. *The Foundations of Research*. London, U.K.: Palgrave Macmillan.

Hallman, H. 2007. "Reassigning the identity of the pregnant and parenting student." *American Secondary Education* 36 (1), 80–98.

Hamilton, B. E., J. A. Martin, and S. J. Ventura. 2012. Births: Preliminary data for 2011. *National Vital Statistics Reports,* 61 (5), 8 (Table 2). http://www.cdc.gov/nchs/data/nvsr/nvsr61/nvsr61_05.pdf.

Hanna, B. 2001. "Negotiating motherhood: The struggles of teenage mothers." *Journal of Advanced Nursing* 34 (4): 456–464.

Hardy, J. B., S. Sharipo, N. Astone, T. L. Miller, and J. Brooks-Gun. 1997. "Adolescent childbearing revisited: The age of inner-city mothers at delivery is a determinant of their children's self-sufficiency at age 27 to 33." *Pediatrics* 100 (5): 802–809.

Harrykissoon, S., V. Rickert, and C. Wiemann. 2002. "Prevalence and patterns of intimate partner violence among adolescent mothers during the postpartum period." *Archives of Pediatrics and Adolescent Medicine* 156: 325–330.

Henretta, J. C. 2007. "Early childbearing, marital status, and women's health and mortality after age 50." *Journal of Health and Social Behavior* 48: 254–266.

Hess, C. R., M. A. Papas, and M. M. Black. 2002. "Resilience among African-American adolescent mothers: Predictors of positive parenting in early infancy." *Journal of Pediatric Psychology* 27 (7): 619–629.

Hofferth, S., and F. Goldscheider. 2010. "Family structure and the transition to early parenthood." *Demography* 47: 415–437.

Hoffman, S. D., and R. A. Maynard, eds. 1997. *Kids Having Kids. Economic Costs and Social Consequences of Teen Pregnancy*. Washington, D.C.: The Urban Institute Press

———. 2008. *Kids having kids: Economic Costs and Social Consequences of Teen Pregnancy*. Washington, D.C.: The Urban Institute Press.

Holub, C., T. Kershaw, K. Ethier, J. B. Lewis, S. Milan, and J. R. Ickovics. 2007. "Prenatal and parenting stress on adolescent maternal adjustment: Identifying a high-risk." *Maternal and Child Health Journal* 11 (2): 153– 159. doi:10.1007/s10995–006–0159-y.

ope, T. L., E. I. Wilder, and T. T. Watt. 2003. "The relationships among adolescent pregnancy, pregnancy resolution, and juvenile delinquency." *Sociological Quarterly* 44 (4): 555–576.

Horwitz, S. M., L. V. Klerman, H. S. Kuo, and J. F. Jekel. 1991. "School-age mothers: predictors of long-term educational and economic outcomes." *Pediatrics* 87 (6): 862–868.

Hubbs-Tait, L. 1986. "Transitions in the Reasoning of Pre- and Early Adolescents: A New Method of Assessment." Paper presented at the 1986 Annual Symposium of the Jean Piaget Society, Philadelphia, PA.

Hunt, G., K. Joe-Laidler, and K. MacKenzie. 2005. "Moving into motherhood: Gang girls and controlled risk." *Youth and Society* 36 (3): 333–373. doi:10.1177/0044118X04266530.

Hurd, N., and M. Zimmerman. 2010. "Natural mentors, mental health, and risk behaviors: A longitudinal analysis of African American adolescents transitioning into adulthood." *American Journal of Community Psychology* 46 (1–2): 36–48.

Hurlburt, N., and A. McDonald. 1997. "Adolescent mother's self-esteem and role identity and their relationship to parenting attitudes." *Adolescence* 32 (127): 639–655.

Ispa, J. M., M. R. Sable, N. Porter, and A. Csizmadia. 2007. "Pregnancy acceptance, parenting stress, and toddler attachment in low-income Black families." *Journal of Marriage and Family* 69: 1–13. doi:10.1111/j.1741-3737.2005.00174.x-i1.

Jacobs, J., and S. Mollborn. 2012. "Early motherhood and the disruption in significant attachments." *Gender and Society* 26 (6): 922–944. doi:10.1177/0891243212459073.

Jaffee, S., A. Caspi, T. E. Moffitt, J. A. Y. Belsky, and P. Silva. 2001. "Why are children born to teen mothers at risk for adverse outcomes in young adulthood? Results from a 20-year longitudinal study." *Development and Psychopathology* 13 (2): 377–397.

Jones, D. J., A. A. Zalot, S. E. Foster, E. Sterrett, and C. Chester. 2007. "A review of childrearing in African American single mother families: The relevance of a coparenting framework." *Journal of Child and Family Studies* 16 (5): 671–683.

Kaiser, M. K., and B. J. Hays. 2004. "The adolescent prenatal questionnaire: Assessing psychosocial facts that influence transition to motherhood." *Health Care for Women International* 25: 5–19. doi:10.1080/07399330490253184.

———. 2005. "Health-risk behaviors in a sample of first-time pregnant adolescents." *Public Health Nursing* 22 (6): 483–493. doi:10.1111/j.0737-1209.2005.220611.x.

————. 2006. "Recruiting and enrolling pregnant adolescents for research." *Issues in Comprehensive Pediatric Nursing* 29: 45–52. doi:10.1080/01460860500523764.

Kaye, D. K. 2008. "Negotiating the transition from adolescence to motherhood: Coping with prenatal and parenting stress in teenage mothers in Mulago hospital, Uganda." *BMC Public Health* 8 (83): 1–6. doi:10.1186/1471-2458-8-83.

Kennedy, A. C. 2006. "Urban adolescent mothers exposed to community, family and partner violence: Prevalence, outcomes, and welfare policy implication." *American Journal of Orthopsychiatry* 76: 44–54.

Kennedy, A. C., and L. Bennett. 2006. "Urban adolescent mothers exposed to community, family and partner violence: Is cumulative violence exposure a barrier to school performance and participation?" *Journal of Interpersonal Violence* 21 (6): 750–773. doi:10.1177/0886260506287314 doi:10.1177/0886260506287314

Kidwell, J., R. M. Dunham, R. A. Bacho, E. Pastorino, and P. Portes. 1995. "Adolescent identity exploration: A test of Erikson's theory of transitional crisis." *Adolescence* 30 (120): 785–793.

Klaw, E. 2008. "Understanding urban adolescent mothers' visions of the future in terms of possible selves." *Journal of Human Behavior in the Social Environment* 18 (4): 441–462.

Knoche, L. L., J. E. Givens, and S. M. Sheridan. 2007. "Risk and protective factors for children of adolescents: Maternal depression and parental sense of competence." *Journal of Child and Family Studies* 16: 684– 695. doi:10.1007/s10826-006-9116-z.

Kotchick, B. A., S. Dorsey, and L. Heller. 2005. "Predictors of parenting among African American single mothers: Personal and contextual factors." *Journal of Marriage and Family* 67: 448–460.

Kreager, D. A., R. L. Matsueda, and E. A. Erosheva. 2010. "Motherhood and criminal desistance in disadvantaged neighborhoods." *Criminology* 48 (1): 221–258.

Lanzi, R. G., S. C. Bert, B. K. Jacobs, and Centers for the Prevention of Child Neglect. 2009. "Depression among a sample of first-time adolescent and adult mothers." *Journal of Child and Adolescent Psychiatric Nursing* 22 (4): 194–202. doi:10.1111/j.1744-6171.2009.00199.x.

Larson, N. C. 2004. "Parenting stress among adolescent mothers in the transition to adulthood." *Child and Adolescent Social Work Journal* 21 (5): 457–475.

Lashley, C. O., S. L. Hans, and L. G. Henson. 2009. "Young African American mother's changing perceptions of their infants during the transition to parenthood." *Infant Mental Health Journal* 30 (5): 477–500.

Leadbeater, B. J. R., and N. Way. 2001. *Growing up Fast: Transitions to Early Adulthood of Inner-City Adolescent Mothers*. Mahwah, NJ: Erlbaum.

Lee, Y. 2009. "Early motherhood and harsh parenting: the role of human, social and cultural capital." *Child Abuse and Neglect* 33: 625–637. doi:10.1016/j.chiabu.2009.02.007.

Leedy, P. D., and J. E. Ormond. 2010. *Practical Research: Planning and Design* (9th ed.). Upper Saddle River, NJ: Pearson.

Lesser, J. and D. Koniak-Griffin. 2000. "The impact of physical and sexual abuse on chronic depression in adolescent mothers." *Journal of Pediatric Nursing* 51: 378–387.

Lesser, J., D. Koniak-Griffin, and N. L. Anderson. 1999. "Depressed adolescent mothers perceptions of their own maternal role." *Maternal Health Nursing* 20: 131–149.

Lesser, J., Oakes, R., and Koniak-Griffin, A. (2003). "Vulnerable adolescent mothers' perception of maternal role and HIV risk." *Health Care for Women International* 24 (2): 513–528.

Letourneau, N. L., M. J. Stewart, and A. K. Barnfather. 2004. "Adolescent-mother: Support needs, resources, and support education intervention." *Journal of Adolescent Health,* 35: 509–525.

Levine, J. A., C. R. Emery, and H. Pollack. 2007. "The well-being of children born to teen mothers." *Journal of Marriage and Family* 59: 105–122.

Levins, M. 1995. "Young Women Who Were Homeless Pregnant Adolescents." Unpublished MSW thesis, California State University, Long Beach.

Lewin, A., S. J. Mitchell, A. Rasmussen, K. Sanders-Phillips, and J. Joseph. 2011. "Do human and social capital protect young African American mothers from depression associated with ethnic discrimination and violence exposure?" *Journal of Black Psychology* 37 (3): 286–310.

Lincoln, Y., and E. Guba. 1985. *Naturalistic Inquiry.* Beverly Hills, CA: Sage.

Lipman, E. L., K. Georgiades, and M. H. Boyle. 2011. "Young adult outcomes of children born to teen mothers: Effects of being born during their teen or later years." *Journal of American Academy of Children and Adolescent Psychiatry* 50 (3): 232–241.

Lodgson, C. M., P. Hertweck, C. Ziegler, and M. Pinto-Foltz. 2008. "Testing a bioecological model to examine social support in postpartum adolescents." *Journal of Nursing Scholarship* 40 (2):116.

Long, M. S. 2009. "Disorganized attachment relationships in infants of adolescent mothers and factors that may augment positive outcomes." *Adolescence* 44 (175): 621–633.

Lounds, J. J., J. G. Borkowski, and T. L. Whitman. 2006. "The potential for child neglect: The case of adolescent mothers and their children." *Child Maltreatment* 11 (3): 281–294.

Low, L. K., K. Martin, C. Sampselle, B. Guthrie, and D. Oakley. 2003. "Adolescents' experiences of childbirth: Contrast with adults." *Journal of Midwifery and Women's Health* 48: 1992–1998.

Luong, M. 2008. "Life after teenage motherhood." *Perspectives on Labour and Income* 20 (2): 41–49.

Mack, L. 2010. *The Philosophical Underpinnings of Educational Research*. Oita, Japan: Ritsumeikan Center for Asia Pacific Studies. http://www.apu.ac.jp/rcaps/uploads/fckeditor/publications/polyglossia/P olyglossia_V19_Lindsay.pdf

Main, M., and E. Hesse, E. 1990. "Parents' unresolved traumatic experiences are related to infant disorganized attachment status: Is frightened and/or frightening parental behavior the linking mechanism?" In M. T. Greenberg, D. Cicchetti, and E. M. Cummings (Eds.), *Attachment in the preschool years: Theory, research, and intervention* (pp. 161–182). The John D. and Catherine T. MacArthur Foundation series on mental health and development. Chicago, IL: University of Chicago Press.

Marcia, J. E. 1976. "Identity six years after: A follow study." *Journal of Youth and Adolescence* 5: 145–160.

Marshall, C., and G. B. Rossman. 2006. *Designing Qualitative Research* (4th ed.). Thousand Oaks, CA: Sage.

Martinez, G., C. E. Copen, and J. C. Abma. 2011. "Teenagers in the United States: Sexual activity, contraceptive use, and childbearing, 2006– 2010." National Survey of Family Growth. *National Vital Health Statics,* 23 (31): 1–35. http://www.cdc.gov/nchs/data/series/sr_23/sr23_031.pdf.

Masten, A., K. Best, and N. Garmezy. 1990. "Resilience and development: contributions from the study of children who overcome adversity." *Development and Psychopathology* 2: 425–444.

Mayberry, L. J., J. A. Horowitz, and E. De Clercq. 2007. "Depression symptom prevalence and demographic risk factors among US women during the first 2 years postpartum." *Journal of Obstetric, Gynecologic, and Neonatal Nursing* 36 (6): 542–549.

McCrary, M. M., and K. Weed. 2005. "Age at first pregnancy, formal operational thought and social support as predictors of identity formation of young mothers." Poster presented at the Society for Research in Adolescence 2005 Annual Meeting, San Francisco, CA.

McDonell, J. R., S. P. Limber, and J. Connor-Godbey. 2007. "Pathways teen mother support project: Longitudinal findings." *Children and Youth Services Review* 29 (7): 840–855.

Meade, C. S., T. S. Kershaw, and J. R. Ickovics. 2008. "The intergenerational cycle of teenage motherhood: an ecological approach." *Health Psychology* 27 (4): 419.

Meadows-Oliver, M. 2006. "Homeless adolescent mothers: A metasynthesis of their life experiences." *Journal of Pediatric Nursing* 21 (4): 340-349. doi:10.1016/j.pedn.2006.02.004.

Meadows-Oliver, M., L. S. Sadler, M. K. Swartz, and P. Ryan-Krause. 2007. "Sources of stress and support and maternal resources of homeless teenage mothers." *Journal of Child and Adolescent Psychiatric Nursing* 20 (2): 116–126.

Mercer, R. T. 1985. "The process of maternal role attainment over the first year." *Nursing Research* 34: 198–204.

———. 1986. *First-Time Motherhood: Experiences From Teens to Forties.*New York, NY: Springer.

———. 2004. "Becoming a mother versus mother role attainment." *Journal of Nursing Scholarship* 36 (3): 226–232. doi:10.1111/j.1547- 5069.2004.04042.x.

———. 2006. "Nursing support of the process of becoming a mother." *Journal of Obstetric, Gynecologic and Neonatal Nursing* 35 (5): 649–651.

Merriam, S. B. 2009. *Qualitative Research: A Guide to Design and Implementation.* San Francisco, CA: Wiley.

Merriwether-de Vries, C. A. 2000. "Adjustment to the Role Motherhood Among Adolescent African American Mothers." Unpublished PhD thesis, Pennsylvania State University, State College.

Meyer, B. W., S. Jain, and K. Canfield-Davis. 2011. "The effect of parenthood education on self-efficacy and parent effectiveness in an alternative high school student population." *The Professional Counselor: Research and Practice* 1 (1): 29–40.

Milan, S., J. R. Ickovics, T. Kershaw, J. Lewis, C. Meade, and K. Etheir. 2004. "Prevalence, course and predictors of emotional distress in pregnant and parenting adolescents." *Journal of Consulting and Clinical Psychology* 72 (2): 328–340.

Mollborn, S. 2007. "Making the best of a bad situation: Material resources and teenage parenthood." *Journal of Marriage and Family,* 69 (1): 92–104.

Moustakas, C. 1994. *Phenomenological Research Methods.* Thousand Oaks, CA: Sage.

National Campaign to Prevent Teen and Unplanned Pregnancy. (2006, December 30). "Science says: The public cost of teen childbearing, 30." http://thenationalcampaign.org/sites/default/files/resource-primary- download/ss30_costs.pdf.

National Campaign to Prevent Teen and Unplanned Pregnancy. (2010, January). Briefly … *Why are the Teen Pregnancy and Birth Rates Increasing?* 29.

National Campaign to Prevent Teen and Unplanned Pregnancy. 2014. *Counting it up: The public costs of teen childbearing.* icon. http://www.thenationalcampaign.org/costs/

Nelson, A. M. 2003. "Transition to motherhood." *Journal of Obstetric, Gynecologic, and Neonatal Nursing* 32 (4): 465–477.

Noria, C. W., K. Weed, and D. A. Keogh. 2007. "The fate of adolescent mothers." In J. Borkowski, J. R. Farris, T. L. Whitman, S. S. Carothers, and Keri Weed (Eds.), *Risk and Resilience: Adolescent Mothers and Their Children Grow Up* (pp. 35-67). Mahwah, NJ: Erlbaum.

Nunes, A. P., and M. G. Phipps. 2012. "Postpartum depression in adolescent and adult mothers: Comparing prenatal risk factors and predictive models." *Maternal and Child Health Journal* 17 (6): 1071–1079. doi:10.1007/s10995-012-1089-5.

Oberlander, S. E., F. M. Shebl, L. S. Magder, and M. M. Black. 2009. "Adolescent mothers leaving multigenerational households." *Journal of Clinical Child and Adolescent Psychology* 38 (1): 62–74.

Oxford, M. L., J. O. Lee, and M. J. Lohr. 2010. "Predicting markers of adulthood among adolescent mothers." *Social Work Research* 34 (1): 33–44.

Oxford, M. L., L. D. Gilchrist, M. J. Lohr, M. R. Gillmore, D. M. Morrison, and S. J. Spieker. 2005. "Life course heterogeneity in the transition from adolescence to adulthood among adolescent mothers." *Journal of Research on Adolescence* 15 (4): 479–504.

Oxford, M. L., O. L. Jungeun, and M. J. Lohr. 2010. "Predicting markers of adulthood among adolescent mothers." *Social Work Research* 34 (1): 33–44.

Passino, A. W., T. L. Whitman, J. G. Borkowski, C. J. Schellenbach, S. E. Maxwell, D. Keogh, and E. Rellinger. 1993. "Personal adjustment during pregnancy and adolescent parenting." *Adolescence* 28 (109): 97–122.

Patton, M. Q. 2002. "Designing qualitative studies." *Qualitative Research and Evaluation Methods* 3: 230–246.

———. 2003. *Qualitative Research and Evaluation Methods* (3rd ed.). Thousand Oaks, CA: Sage.

Perper, K., K. Peterson, and J. Manlove. 2010. *Diploma attainment among teen mothers.* Child Trends Fact Sheet Publication #2010-01. Washington, DC: Child Trends. http://www.childtrends.org/wp- content/uploads/2010/01/child_trends- 2010_01_22_FS_diplomaattainment.pdf

Pinto-Foltz, M. D., M. C. Logsdon, and A. Derrick. 2011. "Engaging adolescent-mothers in a longitudinal mental health intervention study: Challenges and lessons learned." *Issues in Mental Health Nursing* 32: 214–219. doi:10.3109/0 1612840.2010.544841.

Postmus, J. L., C. C. Huang, and A. Mathisen-Stylianou. 2012. "The impact of physical and economic abuse on maternal mental health and parenting." *Children and Youth Services Review* 34: 1922–1928. doi:10.1016/j.childyouth.2012.06.005.

Ramey, C. T., F. A. Campbell, M. Burchinal, M. L. Skinner, D. M. Gardner, and S. L. Ramey. 2000. "Persistent effects of early childhood education on high-risk children and their mothers." *Applied Developmental Science* 4 (1): 2–14.

Reid, V., and M. Meadows-Oliver. 2007. "Postpartum depression in adolescent mothers: An integrative review of the literature." *Journal of Pediatric Health Care* 21 (5): 289–298.

Roche, K. M., M. E. Ensminger, and A. J. Cherlin. 2007. "Variations in parenting and adolescent outcomes among African American and Latino families living in low-income, urban areas." *Journal of Family Issues* 28 (7): 882–909.

Rolfe, A. 2008. "'You've got to grow up when you've got a kid: Marginalized young women's accounts of motherhood." *Journal of Community and Applied Social Psychology* 18 (4): 299–314.

Rosengard, C., L. Pollock, S. Weitzen, A. M. Phipps, and M. G. Phipps. 2006. "Concepts of the advantages and disadvantages of teenage childbearing among pregnant adolescents: A qualitative analysis." *Journal of the American Academy of Pediatrics* 118: 503–510. doi:10.1542/peds.2005-3058.

Rubin, A., and E. Babbie. 2001. *Research Methods for Social Work* (4th ed.) Belmont, CA: Wadsworth/Thomson Learning.

Saewyc, E. M. 2003. "Influential life contexts and environments for out-of-home pregnant adolescents." *Journal of Holistic Nursing* 21(4): 343–367.

Sadler, L. S., and C. Catrone. 1983. "The adolescent parent: A dual developmental crisis." *Journal of Adolescent Health Care* 4 (2): 100–105.

Sadler, L. S., and A. Cowlin. 2003. "Moving into parenthood: A program for new adolescent mothers combining parent education with creative physical activity." *Journal for Specialists in Pediatric Nursing* 8: 62–70. doi:10.1111/j.1744-6155.2003.tb00188.x.

Sadler, L. S., M. K. Swartz, P. Ryan-Krause, V. Seitz, M. Meadows-Oliver, M. Grey, and D. A. Clemmens. 2007. "Promising outcomes in teen mothers enrolled in a school-based parent support program and child care center." *Journal of School Health* 77: 121–130. doi:10.1111/j.1746-1561.2007.00181.x.

Sangalang, B., R. P. Barth, and J. S. Painter. 2006. "First-birth outcomes and timing of second birth: A statewide case management." *Health and Social Work* 31 (1): 54–62.

Sangalang, B. B. 2006. "Teenage mothers in parenting programs: Exploring welfare outcomes during early transition to parenthood." *Families in Society* 87(1): 105–111.

Sauls, D. 2004. "Adolescent perception of supporting during labor." *The Journal of Perinatal Education* 13 (1): 36–43.

Schmidt, R. M., C. M. Wiemann, V. I. Rickert, and E. B. Smith. 2006. "Moderate to severe depressive symptoms among adolescent mothers followed four years postpartum." *Journal of Adolescent Health* 38 (6): 712–718.

Schwandt, T. A. 2007. *The Sage Dictionary of Qualitative Inquiry.* Los Angeles, CA: Sage.

Secco, M. L., and M. E. Moffatt. 2003. "Situational, maternal, and infant influences on parenting stress among adolescent mothers." *Issues in Comprehensive Pediatric Nursing* 26 (2): 103–122.

Secco, M. L., S. Profit, E. Kennedy, A. Walsh, N. Letourneau, and M. Stewart, 2007. "Factors affecting postpartum depressive symptoms of adolescent mothers." *Journal of Obstetric, Gynecologic, and Neonatal Nursing* 36 (1): 47–54.

Shanok, A. F., and L. Miller. 2005. "Fighting and depression among poor pregnant adolescents." *Journal of Reproductive and Infant Psychology* 23 (3): 207–218.

———. 2007a. "Stepping up to motherhood among inner-city teens." *Psychology of Women Quarterly* 31: 252–261.

———. 2007b. "Depression and treatment with inner city pregnant and parenting teens." *Archives of Women's Mental Health* 10: 199–210. doi:10.1007/s00737-007-0194-8.

Sieger, K., and K. Renk. 2007. "Pregnant and parenting adolescents: A study of ethnic identity, emotional and behavioral functioning, child characteristics, and social support." *Journal Youth Adolescence* 36 (6): 567–581. doi 10.1007/s10964-007-9182-6.

Silk, J., and D. Romero. 2013. "The role of parents and families in teen pregnancy prevention: An analysis of programs and policies." *Journal of Family Issues* 35 (4). Advance online publication. doi:10.1177/0192513X13481330.

Singh S., and J. E. Darroch. 2000. "Adolescent pregnancy and childbearing: Levels and trends in developed countries." *Family Planning Perspective* 32: 114–123.

SmithBattle, L. 1996. "Intergenerational ethics of caring for teenage mothers and their children." *Family Relations* 45: 56-64.

———. 2007. "Legacies of advantage and disadvantage: The case of teen Mothers." *Public Health Nursing* 24 (5): 409–423.

———. 2009. "Reframing the risks and losses." *The American Journal of Maternal Child Nursing* 34 (2): 122–142.

———. 2010. "Listening with care to teen mothers and their families." In G. Chan, K. Brykczynski, R. Malone, and P. Benner (Eds.), *Interpretive Phenomenology in Health Care Research* (217-241). Indianapolis, IN: Sigma Theta Tau International.

———. 2012. "Moving policies upstream to mitigate the social determinants of early childbearing." *Public Health Nursing* 29 (5): 444– 454. doi:10.1111/j.1525-1446.2012.01017.x.

———. 2013. "Reducing the stigmatization of teen mothers." *The American Journal of Maternal Child Nursing* 38 (4): 235–241. doi:10.1097/NMC.0b013e3182836bd4.

SmithBattle, L., and V. Leonard. 2012. "Inequities compounded explaining variations in the transition to adulthood for teen mothers' offspring." *Journal of Family Nursing* 18 (3): 409–431.

Sommer, K., T. L. Whitman, J. G. Borkowski, C. Schellenbach, S. Maxwell, and D. Keogh. 1993. "Cognitive readiness and adolescent parenting." *Developmental Psychology,* 29 (2): 389–398.

Sommer, K. S., T. L. Whitman, J. G. Borkowski, D. M. Gondoli, J. Burke, S. E. Maxwell, and K. Weed. 2000. "Prenatal maternal predictors of cognitive and emotional delays in children of adolescent mothers." *Adolescence* 35 (137): 87–112.

Steinberg, L., and A. S. Morris. 2001. "Adolescent Development." *Annual Review Psychology* 52: 83–110.

Stevenson, W., K. I. Maton, and D. M. Teti. 1999. "Social support, relationship quality, and well-being among pregnant adolescents." *Journal of Adolescence* 22 (1): 109–121.

Stiles, S. A. 2010. "Case study of an intervention to enhance maternal sensitive in adolescent mothers." *Journal of Obstetric, Gynecologic and Neonatal Nursing* 39: 723–733. doi:10.1111/j.1552-6909.2010.01183.x.

Stones, C. R. 1979. "Research: Toward a phenomenological praxis." In Dreyer Kruger, *An introduction to phenomenological psychology* (pp. 113– 139). Pittsburgh, PA: Duquesne University Press.

Sumner, L. A., L. Wong, C. D. Schetter, H. F. Myers, and M. Rodriguez. 2012. "Predictors of posttraumatic stress disorder symptoms among low-income Latinas during pregnancy and postpartum." *Psychological Trauma, Theory, Research, Practice, and Policy* 4 (2): 196–203.

Swedish, K. A., A. Rothenberg, K. Fuchs, and G. Rosenberg. 2010. "Successful life navigation by former participants in a group for pregnant and parenting teens." *Vulnerable Children and Youth Studies* 5: 310–321. doi:10.1080/174501 28.2010.507806.

Taylor, R. D., E. I. Lopez, M. Budescu, and R. K. McGill. 2012. "Parenting practices and adolescent internalizing and externalizing problems: Moderating effects of socially demanding kin relations." *Journal of Child and Family Studies* 21 (3): 474–485

Taylor, R. D. 2011. "Kin support and parenting practices among low-income African American mothers: Moderating effects of mothers' psychological adjustment." *Journal of Black Psychology* 37 (1): 3–23.

Taylor, R. D., E. Seaton, and A. Dominguez. 2008. "Kinship support, family relations, and psychological adjustment among low-income African-American mothers and adolescents." *Journal of Research on Adolescence* 18 (1): 1–22.

Taylor, R. D. 2010. "Risk and resilience in low-income African American families: Moderating effects of kinship social support." *Cultural Diversity and Ethnic Minority Psychology* 16 (3): 344.

Terry-Humen, E., J. Manlove, and S. Cottingham. 2006. "Trends and recent estimates: Sexual activity among US teens." Child Trends Research Brief. Publication # 2006-08. Washington, DC: Child Trends.

Thompson, T., and C. R. Massat. 2005. "Experiences of violence, post-traumatic stress, academic and behavior problems of urban African American children." *Child and Adolescent Social Work Journal* 22 (5–6): 367–392.

Turley, R. N. 2003. "Are children of young mothers disadvantaged because of their mother's age or family background?" *Child Development* 74 (2), 465–474.

Ventura, S. J., and T. J. Matthews, and B. E. Hamilton, P. D. Sutton, J. C. Abma, and National Center for Health Statistics, CDC. 2011. "Adolescent pregnancy and childbirth-United States, 1991–2008." In CDC health disparities and inequalities report, United States, 2011. *MMWR Surveillance Summaries* 60 (Suppl): 105–108. http://www. cdc.gov.mmwr/pdf/other/su6001.pdf

Virginia Department of Health (VDH), Center for Health Statistics. (n.d.). Statistical reports and tables. Data tables. Births, pregnancies, induced terminations, teenage pregnancies, 2009. www.vdh.virginia.gov/healthstats/stats.htm.

Wargo, W. G. 2011. *Secrets and Tips for Dissertation Completion.* Raleigh, NC: Lulu Press.

Whitman, T. L., J. G. Borkowski, D. A. Keogh, and K. Weed. 2001. *Interwoven Lives: Adolescent Mothers and Their Children.* Mahwah, NJ: Erlbaum.

Wright, P., and A. A. Davis. 2008. "Adolescent parenthood through educators' eyes: Perceptions of worries and provision of support." *Urban Education* 43 (6): 671–695. doi:10.1177/0042085907311827.

Xie, H., B. D. Cairns, and R. B. Cairns. 2001. "Predicting teen motherhood and teen fatherhood: Individual characteristics and peer affiliations." *Social Development* 10 (4): 488–511.

Yampolskaya, S., E. C. Brown, and A. C. Vargo. 2004. "Assessment of teen pregnancy interventions among middle school youth." *Child and Adolescent Social Work Journal* 21: 69–83.

Zastrow, C., and K. Kirst-Ashman. 2006. *Understanding human behavior and the social environment* (7th ed.). Belmont, CA: Thomason-Brooks/Cole.

Zimmer, M. A., L. Tuttle, E. Kieffer, E. Parker, C. H. Caldwell, and K. I. Maton. 2001. "Psychosocial Outcomes of Urban African American Adolescents Born to Teenage Mothers." *Journal of Community Psychology* 29 (5): 779–805. doi:10.1023/A:1010469218757.

Interview Questions

1. Describe your life before you became pregnant.
2. Describe what your life was like after having your baby.
3. At what point did you realize that you were a mother? Describe your feelings at the particular moment.
4. What impact did having a baby have on your life and how did you handle the impact?
5. Describe the feelings or emotions you experienced in your new role of being a mother.
6. What significant element(s) helped you during your transitional phase from being a teen to becoming a mother? Describe the element(s) and how it (they) helped you.
7. What would you say was the most challenging part about being a teen mother, and how did you overcome the challenging situations?
8. Describe a moment that made you feel proud of yourself.
9. What significant changes did you make in your life once you had your baby?

Panel Member Rating

Questions 1, 3, and 8 received high ratings from all panelists; however, comments also suggested that the questions were not aligned with the primary research questions. Those questions were revised.

Questions 4, 5, and 9 received fair ratings; however, the questions were noted by three panelists as being too similar to other questions, and one panelist stated the questions were too ambiguous.

Questions 2, 6, and 7 were noted by all panelists as repetitive and too broad, which would yield varying results. All of the questions received a 1 rating.

Overall, three of the four panelists recommended that all of the questions be revised to be aligned with the research questions. The initial nine questions were reduced to seven questions that were better aligned with the two research questions. All of the panelists suggested keeping the questions positive. The results of this field test were revised research questions, in which all panelists scored the new questions with high ratings.

CURRICULUM VITAE

Kateresea L. Ford
Glen Allen, VA-683-8608

Email: drkatford@gmail.com
Facebook: facebook.com/drkatford
LinkedIn: linkedin.com/in/katereseaford
Website: www.drkatford.com

Statement of Teaching Philosophy

I believe that every person has the capability to learn and that the instructor has the responsibility and opportunity to ensure delivery of content to help students achieve personal and professional goals. Each individual learns differently and the faculty member's ability to be innovative and help students master content is vital in the course room. I enjoy helping students become more prepared for the workforce and equipped to help others. Facilitators have the bonus of being able to expand their own knowledge as they teach, and knowing they made a difference in another's life and empowered a student is highly rewarding.

Personal Attributes

Highly qualified educator with seven years of college-level teaching experience in both online and on-ground environments.

Dedicated and detail oriented professional with extensive counseling and mental health experience, with a strong desire to apply this commitment and dedication to higher education.

Experienced leader with highly developed research and organizational skills.

Excellent communication and interpersonal skills, with the ability to work effectively with individuals from diverse backgrounds.

Expertise in counseling psychology, human services and counseling education, with the desire and willingness to share my knowledge and experiences with students.

Teaching Experience

Ashford University   July 2015
Associate Online Faculty, San Diego CA

Virginia State University   January 2012 – April 2014
Guest Lecturer, Petersburg, VA

Provide lectures on fundamentals of mental health and effective clinical treatment to traditional and nontraditional college students.

Conduct lectures on ethics and clinical decision making strategies twice a week with up to 25 students per class.

Courses Taught:

SOWK 340 02 Social Welfare Policy Analysis
This course introduces students to a framework for the analysis of social problems and services, and focuses upon the variables that shape human service delivery systems. Application of analytical skills to a social policy is a required component of the course. This course is writing intensive.

Social Work 495: Advanced Topics in Social Work

This course focuses on a selected topic on a controversial issue and social work practice that reflect current trends in the field of social work. The course may be repeated for credit with different topics with the consent of the department.

Strayer University   August 2003 – April 2007
Adjunct Faculty, Arlington, VA

Taught introduction to psychology and individual of society courses online using E-College and providing discussion questions, live chat opportunities, online study sessions, and supplemental course materials for university catering to over 54,0000 adult learners.

Worked with traditional and non-traditional college age students in classroom setting five times per week with up to 30 students per class.

Utilized multiple methods of teaching to capture various learning styles to ensure student success and maintained 3.8 out of 4.0 student satisfaction scores.

Created syllabuses as well as class materials and tests for courses and assisted with course development and revision.

Courses Taught:

PSY 100 Psychology of Adjustment
This course emphasizes how psychological concepts can be applied to everyday life. It covers prominent theories in major areas of psychology and discusses their relevance to one's life.

The course discusses strategies for improving coping skills, handling stress, building self-esteem, enhancing interpersonal communication, and understanding relationships. Workplace issues, human sexuality, mental health and physical health are also covered.

PSY 105 Introduction to Psychology
May be taken in place of PSY 100
Introduces psychology as a human and scientific endeavor. Includes examination of concepts and methods in learning, motivation, development, personality, and social behavior.

PSY 110 Social Psychology
Focuses on major theories in social psychology and the most recent research in the field. Topics include gender, interpersonal attraction, aggression, and prosocial behavior.

Professional Positions in Education

Creative Youth Concepts, Inc.   June 2008 – April 2015
Clinical Director Richmond, VA

Supervise 15-25 clinical staff providing training, work assignment and review, performance evaluations and employee discipline as necessary.

Provide weekly clinical supervision to which staff trained on clinical approaches to working with their clients.

Identify staff training needs and develop workshops or recommend training programs to enhance their performance, including development of casework plans, case management and case monitoring.

Provide weekly case reporting, assist staff by identifying clinical issues related to referrals, assist staff in identifying appropriate resources and treatment options.

Developed human rights policy and procedures for state licensed organizations.

Posted job openings on internet job boards and newspaper, conducted employment interviews, made hiring decisions, conducted performance evaluations, and managed employee discipline, promotions, and termination

Richmond Public School   August 1998 – August 2006
Middle School Guidance Counselor, Richmond, VA

Taught life and social skills to urban youth ages 11-18 with various academic and behavioral issues.

Provided guidance and counseling to youth ages 10-18 for 200 students.

Created and implemented master schedule for school.

Provided schedules for teachers and students.

Testing Coordinator- Conducted standardized state testing.

Served as Chair for Child Study (Exceptional Education) Team.

Prepared and reviewed Individual Service Plans and 504 Plan for students with disabilities.

Coordinated Alternative Education program for at-risk and over aged students.

Coordinator of work-study program for at-risk youth.

Conducted bi-weekly counseling groups for students.

Professional Experience

Creative Youth Concepts, Inc.   October 2003 – April 2015
Chief Administrative Officer, Richmond, VA

Oversaw daily operations of organization providing outreach, educational, and therapeutic services to youth and families and established best practices programming for staff

Managed, mentored, and motivated team of up to 65 team members including chief executive officers, clinical directors, program directors, teachers, and residential workers utilizing social and participative leadership styles.

Establish company priorities; participate in program planning, develop recommendations and assist with development and implementation of program objectives, policies, procedures and standards,

Managed quality assurance and ensured compliance with state laws, regulations, and statutes,

Monitored daily clinical practices and coordinated policies changes thereto; monitor and evaluate program effectiveness.

Developed and executed policy and procedures for state licensed community mental health organization

Developed and executed policy and procedures for licensed residential group home for teen-mothers.

Developed human rights policy and procedures for state licensed organizations.

Oversaw the development and management of educational programming, mental health development, and hands-on programming delivery, instruction and training.

Coordinated clinical programming with local service providing organizations, local schools, department of social services, and department of juvenile justice and community mental health agencies.

Posted job openings on internet job boards and newspaper, conducted employment interviews, made hiring decisions, conducted performance evaluations, and managed employee discipline, promotions, and termination.

Entrepreneurial Experience

Delta House Residential Services March 2004 – January 2015
Chief Executive Officer, Richmond, VA

Established two state licensed residential group home for pregnant and parenting teen-mothers, which included, creating policy and procedures, human right policies and procedures, standard operational protocols and manual use to effectively execute programming and services

Conceptualized and executed therapeutic program for teen-mothers who were in fostercare, homeless, on probation with juvenile justice system, or parental placement, providing housing, counseling and daycare services.

Directed clinical program for teens and single mothers while supervising 17 residential program workers and created standards of operations for program implementation.

Administered budgets and programs simultaneously for two companies, successfully reducing bottom-line costs by 5% through service streamlining, employee retention, and product efficiency.

Created and established strategic planning, mission, and policy of programs and implemented staff and management training that reinforced visions, plans, and challenges.

Creative Counseling and Consulting Concepts, Inc.   June 2012 – Present

Licensed Professional Counselor/Clinical Supervisor, Richmond, VA

Provide clinical services clients ranging from ages 4 to 65.

Provide individual and family therapy for youth and adults, with a caseload of 10-15 clients utilizing client center techniques.

Provide therapeutic interventions for EAP clients to include, anger and stress management, life coaching and family intervention strategies.

Facilitate 2-3 therapeutic groups weekly.

Ensure confidential case files are maintained on each client.

Formal Education

PhD, General Human Services   2014
Capella University, Minneapolis, MN

MEd, Counseling Education 1998
Virginia State University, Petersburg, VA

BS, Psychology 1996
Virginia Commonwealth University, Richmond, VA

State License and Education Certifications

Licensed Professional Counselor, Virginia State 2012
Board of Professionals

Advance Graduate Certification in Human Services 2008
Nova Southeastern University, Miami, FL

Postgraduate Professional License, Endorsements in 1997
Administration and Supervision,
PreK-12, and School Counselor
Virginia Department of Education

Business/Technical Training and Certifications

Certified Clinical Mental Health Counselor 2015
(CCMHC), National Board Certified Counselor

Approved Clinical Supervisor (ACS), Center for 2015
Credentialing and Education

Registered Play Therapist (RPT), National 2013
Association of Play Therapist

National Certified Counselor (NCC), National 2012
Board Certified Counselor

Co-Parenting Trainer, Supreme Court of Virginia	2012
Nurturing Parenting Trainer Training	2011
Master Trainer, Arise Life Skills Curriculum	2010
Trainer Understanding Frameworks of Poverty, Aha! Process	2009

Memberships and Affiliations

Member   2006 – Present
American Counseling Association

Member   2006 – Present
Virginia Counseling Association

Member   2012 – Present
American Play Therapist Association

Member   2013-Present
Central Virginia African American Chambers of Commerce

Community Service and Leadership

Mentored Business Leader   2012 - 2014
City of Richmond Office of Minority Business Development/
Capital One Mentorship Program
Richmond, VA

Committee Member   2008
Local State Human Rights, Richmond, VA

Active Member of Delta Sigma Theta   1995-Present
Sorority, Inc.
Richmond Alumnae Chapter
Member of Executive Board
Chair of Infinite Scholars Scholarship Fair
Chair of Step Team
Co-Chair Delta Academy

Professional and Scholarly Presentations

Understanding Community Mental Health,   2012 – Present
Community Providers Meeting
Creative Youth Concepts, Inc., Richmond, VA

Understanding Mental Health Disorders in   2010 – 2012
Urban Youth
Richmond Public Schools, MLK Middle School, Richmond, VA

Maintaining Professional Ethics with Today's Youth,   2010
Youth & Residential Provider Symposium
Area Community Providers Network, Richmond, VA

Understanding Needs of Urban Youth in Poverty,   2009 – 2010
King Middle School
Martin Luther King Middle School Teachers, Richmond, VA

Dynamics of Teen Mothers, Teen Pregnancy   2008
Prevention Partnerships
Teen Parenting Coalition, Richmond, VA

Conferences Attended

Virginia Counselor Association   2013
Fredericksburg, VA

Attendee, Healthy Teen Network Conference   2011
Healthy Teen Network, Pittsburgh, PA

Residencies and Colloquia

Capella University Dissertation Writing Workshop   2012
Chicago, IL

Capella University Colloquia   2011
Arlington, VA

Capella University Colloquia   2009
Jacksonville, FL

Publications

Ford, K. (2012). *Negotiating identities: The transition to motherhood in young urban adolescent mothers*. (Doctoral dissertation, Capella University).

Ford, K. (2015). *Negotiating Identities: The Transition To Motherhood In Young Urban Adolescent Mothers*. Richmond, VA: D. Boyer Consulting Publisher.

Awards and Honors

Member Virginia Commonwealth University   2012 – Present
Psychology Alumni Board

| City of Richmond Office of Minority Business | 2013 |
| Development | |

Emerging Business Leader

| Community Volunteer Award | |
| Henrico County Public Schools | 2011, 2012 |

| Volunteer Award | 2008-2010 |
| Virginia Randolph High School | |

| Outstanding New Business | |
| Richmond Economic Development Corporation | 2005 |

| Outstanding New Teacher Award | 1998 |
| Richmond Public Schools | |

| Leadership Award | 1999, 2000-2005 |
| Richmond Public Schools | |

Highly Competent Subject Matters

Software:
  Microsoft Word
  Microsoft Excel
  Microsoft Publisher

Learning Management Systems:
  E-College
  Blackboard
  WebCT 7
  ASIST

Subject Matter Expert:

Psychology
Counseling Psychology
General Human Services
Counseling
Counseling Education
Models of Clinical Supervision
Ethics in Practice
Individual Counseling
Academic Study and Writing
Marriage and Family Therapy
Multicultural Issues in Counseling
Research Methods
Methods and Analysis of Quantitative Research
Methods and Analysis of Qualitative Research
Research in Adult Human Development and Behavior
Ethic and Cultural Awareness
Diversity in the Workplace
Epistemology of Practice Knowledge
Families, Systems and Health Care
Social Science Research
Health Care Strategic Planning and Management
Quantitative Research Methods in Human Services
Ethics and Decision Making in Health Care
Marriage and Family Systems

www.ingramcontent.com/pod-product-compliance
Lightning Source LLC
Chambersburg PA
CBHW030430290526
45786CB00001B/213